D0528604

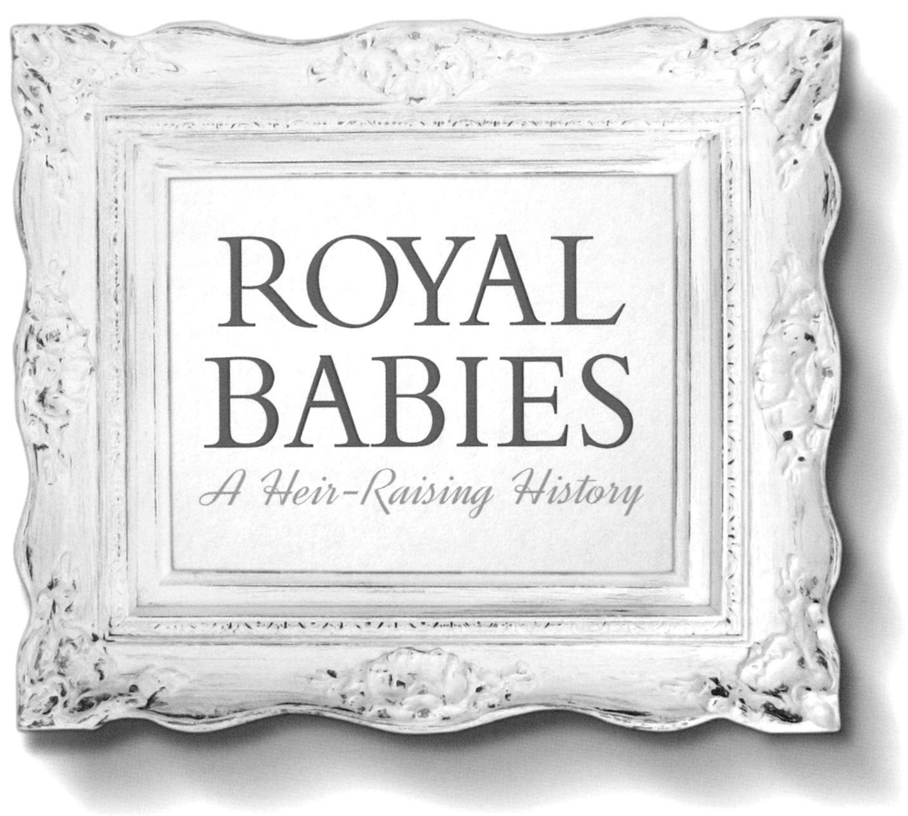

Alison James

First Published Danann Publishing Ltd 2018

CAT NO: DAN0376

Photography courtesy of

Getty images:

Print Collector
Hulton Royals Collection
W. and D. Downey / Stringer
Hulton Archive / Stringer
Mansell / Contributor
Culture Club
George Rinhart
Hulton Deutsch
Bettmann
Royal Photographic Society
Universal History Archive
Topical Press Agency / Stringer

Popperfoto
Fox Photos / Stringer
AFP
Keystone / Stringer
Anwar Hussein
David Levenson
Tim Graham
Wpa Pool / Pool
Julian Parker
Carl Court / Stringer
John Stillwell/AFP
Chris Jackson

Marty Melville / Stringer
Ben A. Pruchnie / Stringer
Ben Stansall
Justin Tallis/AFP
Christian Charisius
Mark Cuthbert
Franziska Krug
Universal History Archive
Heritage Images
Ullstein Bild Dtl.
Kirby / Stringer

Other images, Wiki Commons

Book layout & design Darren Grice at Ctrl-d

Copy Editor Juliette O'Neill

Made in EU.

ISBN: 978-1-912332-14-4

Contents

Introduction

Welcome to Royal Babies – a Heir-Raising History.

Within these pages are tales of Royal pregnancies, births and babyhoods from medieval times up to the present day. Stories of hope and fear, joy and pain, triumph and tragedy, humour and hubris, life and death . . . set against the backdrop of the British Royal Family, the world's most famous monarchy. Real-life stories played out over the centuries in the history of begetting, carrying, bearing and bringing up babies of the Blood Royal. It is a sensational, often surreal, kind of soap opera — but one with a sovereign spin. But, in parts, it is also a social history of how we, as human beings, came into being, were born and survived through infancy and childhood. It maps and mirrors the evolution of these life stages over time — from the 15th century Margaret Beaufort being tossed in the air while in labour as midwives attempted to turn the breech baby who would be the future King Henry VII to the Duchess of Cambridge reportedly wishing for a very 21st century non-interventionist home birth for her third child.

Where Royalty lead, the rest of us have traditionally followed. The Duchess of Cambridge, like her late mother-in-law, Princess Diana, is a Queen of trendsetters. Catherine's hair, make-up and fashion styles are copied the world over and the designs she wears sell out within seconds. It is the same with her maternity wardrobe, how she conducts her pregnancies, the decisions made regarding the births of her babies, the names chosen for them, how she and William raise their family. . . right down to the cute clothes worn by their offspring, which sell out within minutes of them being seen on the children. It was ever thus. The pram, or perambulator as it was originally known, became popular in the 1840s when Queen Victoria purchased three, ready-made baby carriages from Hitchings of Ludgate Hill. From then on, pram manufacturers adopted a tradition of labelling their ranges with names such as '*Queen*', '*Princess*', '*Royal' and* '*Duchess*' — and the '*Balmoral*' and '*Kensington*' prams made by Silver Cross are still in production today. On a more serious note, in the field of obstetrics, Royalty have also blazed a trail. In the 1620s, Queen Henrietta Maria, consort of King Charles I, was the first woman in the world to give birth assisted by the then top secret gynaecological invention that were forceps. Over 200 years later Queen Victoria became one of the first women ever to be administered chloroform for labour pain relief, while her husband Prince Albert was, very unusually for the time, at her bedside on each of the nine occasions she gave birth.

Accompanied by stunning images of Royal babies past and present, this gloriously gossipy, heir-raising history reveals fascinating fact-filled, maternity minutiae of the monarchical kind. Which Royal new mum, for instance, received an apple green Mini convertible as a post-partum '*push present*' while one Tudor mother-to-be couldn't stop eating apples during her pregnancy? Which Royal matriarch was so detached from her elder sons she had no inkling they were abused by their nanny? Which Royal father was more responsible for child rearing than his regal wife? Why were red-headed wet-nurses frowned upon? Which Queen attempted to stave off the pangs of childbirth by magic? And which baby Prince pee'd on his nanny at his christening? '*Royal Babies — a Heir Raising History*' reveals everything you've ever wanted to know about how British Royals throughout history

have gone forth, multiplied, survived and thrived . . .

Queen Anne Boleyn's craving during pregnancy in 1533

'She has inestimable wild desire to eat apples, such as she has never had in her life before'

Before Victoria

It takes a strong woman, whatever the hue of her blood, to keep it together during the heavy swell that is pregnancy and childbirth. Before the days of basic hygiene and sanitation, it was scarily life-threatening even if you were a Queen. The days when a delivery suite was an airless, wooden-panelled prison, when a labouring lady's waters were broken with the sharp edge of a coin or a midwife's grubby finger nail. When Caesarean sections were only performed on dying women so that their unborn babies might survive, when a loss of blood always meant a loss of life and any kind of pain relief was regarded as sinful. Delicate Royal ladies were thought to suffer more in childbirth than lower-born women. It was a class thing - the posher you were, the harder you had it. There was additional pressure on labouring Royal ladies. The fate of a Royal dynasty may well depend on the birth of a hale and hearty boy child. This was a Royal wife's primary purpose in life, the reason they had been married to a Prince or King in the first place. There was evidence everywhere — in history and overseas - of dynasties dying out because no heir had been produced. Under such pressure, it wasn't always easy for a Queen to maintain her position or status. *'Get thee to a nunnery!'* was no idle threat. And one Queen famously lost her head. . .

Conceiving a baby, let alone carrying one to full term, has been problematic to some of our Queens throughout history. There is no record of Queen Berengaria, the Spanish wife of 12th century monarch Richard the Lionheart, ever conceiving. The fact that they never saw each other might have had something to do with it. Apart from one brief spell when Berengaria joined Richard on crusade, throughout their eight-year marriage they were never in the same country at the same time — let alone the same bed. As Richard is thought to have been gay, the bottom line is that he probably preferred a different kind of queen! The last three wives of Henry VIII — Anne of Cleves, Katherine Howard and Katherine Parr — never fell pregnant by their Royal sire, most likely because Henry was totally impotent by the time of his fourth marriage. His second wife, Anne Boleyn, had hinted that he had a problem and her treacherous sister-in-law, Jane Boleyn, revealed this at Anne's stumped-up trial for adultery in 1536. But by the time Henry was married to third wife, Jane Seymour, he seemed concerned about his own virility, telling henchman Thomas Cromwell that, '*he felt himself already growing old and doubted whether he should have any child by the Queen*'. The 17th century King Charles II was definitely not impotent, having fathered upwards of 16 illegitimate children, and yet his wife of 23 years, Catherine of Braganza, managed to conceive just once — and the pregnancy ended in miscarriage. Her infertility was savagely gossiped about at court and she regularly visited the spas at Tunbridge Wells and Bath, hoping the waters would work some magic.

Right:

'The Five Eldest Children of Charles I',1637. Artist: Anthony van Dyck

She even resorted to placing live pigeons at her feet when she was in bed, an old wives' tale said to increase the chances of conception. Not surprisingly, it didn't work and can hardly have inflamed Charles' ardour, either. The years went by and the King considered having the marriage annulled but he chose not to, possibly because long-suffering Catherine put up with his relentless philandering. By contrast, other Royal ladies had no trouble conceiving a child. Catherine of Aragon, first wife of the then virile Henry VIII, fell pregnant several times — although only one of her children survived through babyhood and beyond. The Stuart Queen Anne was pregnant a record breaking 17 times yet tragically few of these pregnancies went full term and of those that did, no children survived beyond childhood. On a happier note, George III's Queen, Charlotte, became pregnant 15 times — none of which ended in miscarriage or still birth — and 13 of her children reached adulthood. The signs and symptoms of pregnancy are timeless — the cessation of menstruation, tender breasts, possible sickness and, later in pregnancy, feeling the baby move. In the past, this last symptom, known as '*quickening*', was the ultimate sure sign that a baby was on the way. There were also cravings for certain foods, experienced by some Royal ladies. Elizabeth Woodville, Edward IV's Queen, couldn't get enough of the sea vegetable Samphire when carrying daughter Cecily in 1469. In Spring 1533, when pregnant with the future Elizabeth 1, Queen Anne Boleyn was heard announcing that she had '*an inestimable wild desire to eat apples, such as she has never had in her life before,*' and that the King had told her it must be because she was with child. Henry's third wife, Jane Seymour liked to gorge on quail and cucumber when she was pregnant with the future Edward VI in 1537. Henry had crates of the game bird shipped in from Calais to satisfy his blossoming wife's cravings while her step daughter, Mary, brought Jane cucumbers from her own garden to crunch through.

Until the 15th century, pregnant ladies — both blue and red-blooded — wore their regular clothes when pregnant. Back then robes were made from flowing lengths of fabric and were seamless rather than cut and

Left:

James, (1633 - 1701), the second son of King Charles I, as Prince James, Duke of York. He is the future James II, King of England, and James VII, King of Scotland. 'The Stuart Baby', by Sir Anthony Van Dyck

Right:

Edward VI (1537-1553) King of England and Ireland from 1547. Son of Henry VIII and his third wife, Jane Seymour. Always a sickly child, he died of natural causes in 1554 aged 16

sewn to shape. But from the 1500s onwards, the garments of well-to-do women began to hug the figure more and a pregnant lady would have had her seams let out to allow for expansion. Most Royal ladies would do their upmost to disguise their condition for as long as they could — but not Queen Anne Boleyn. She was six months pregnant with Elizabeth when she was crowned Queen in a lavish four-day ceremony in late Spring 1533. She wished to show off her bump to prove that Henry VIII had been right to break with Rome in order to marry her. Anne, whom Archbishop Cranmer noted was '*big with child*', wore a gown of white cloth of gold for her ceremonial entry into London and an extra panel of cloth had to be sewn into the dress to accommodate her thickening waist.

As due dates approached, certain customs were adhered to regarding the births of Royal babies. For over 500 years from Norman times un the 17th century a Royal mother-to-be would withdraw into her '*lying in*' chamber approximately six weeks before she was due. She would not emerge again until her '*churching*' ceremony, at which she would be '*cleansed*' of childbirth, a month after the birth. Once inside the chamber, shutters and windows would be closed, key holes stopped up, and tapestries hung to ensure the room was airtight, therefore making it impossible for evil spirits to enter. Childbirth was a strictly '*Women Only*' affair for the Royal mother-to-be. Midwives rather than physicians would deliver the Regal offspring and these women, who had learnt their trade by assisting at births from childhood rather than by reading text books, would attend Royal birth after Royal birth. In the chamber, many other women would also have been present — ladies-in-waiting, wet-nurses, dry nurses, nurses-in-waiting, rockers of the Royal cradle, family members and friends. . . These gangs of women were known as '*God's Sibs*', as in '*God's Siblings*' which over time became abbrievated to '*Gossips*'.

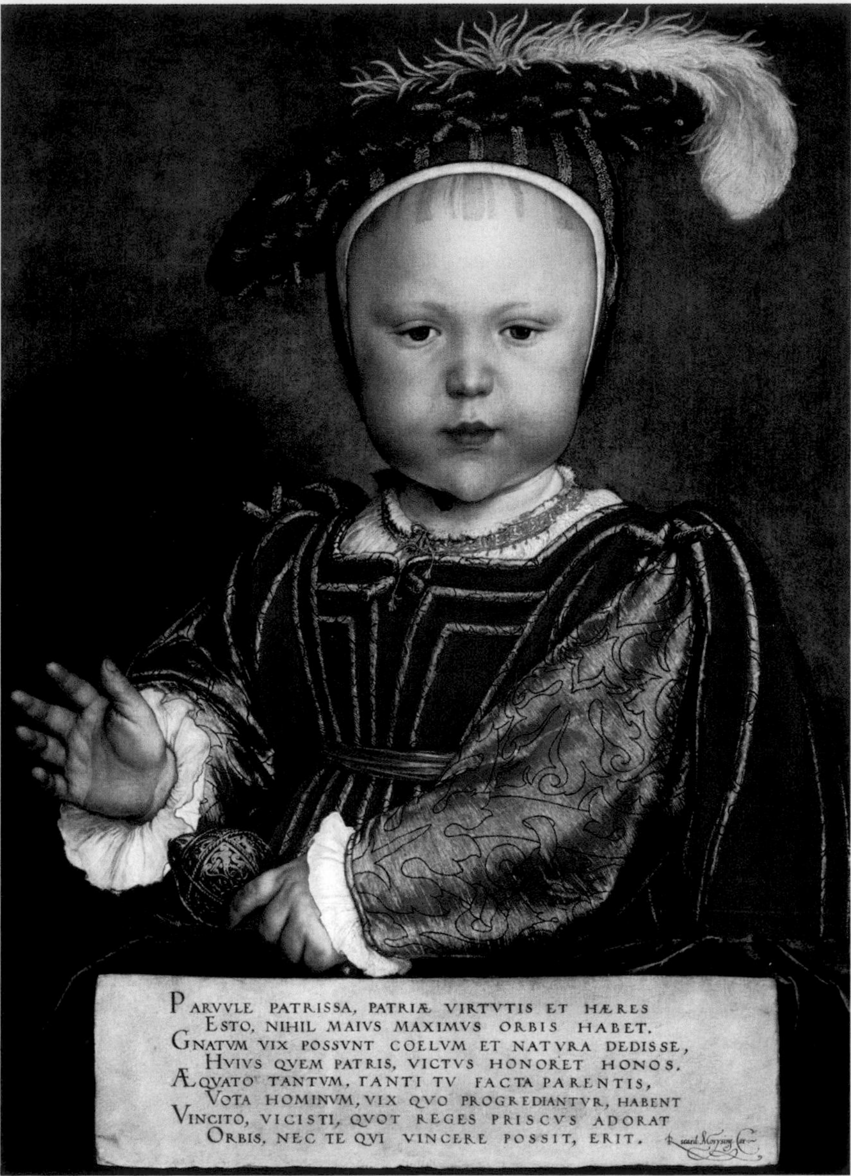

PARVVLE PATRISSA, PATRIÆ VIRTVTIS ET HÆRES
ESTO, NIHIL MAIVS MAXIMVS ORBIS HABET.
GNATVM VIX POSSVNT COELVM ET NATVRA DEDISSE,
HVIVS QVEM PATRIS, VICTVS HONORET HONOS.
ÆQVATO TANTVM, TANTI TV FACTA PARENTIS,
VOTA HOMINVM, VIX QVO PROGREDIANTVR, HABENT
VINCITO, VICISTI, QVOT REGES PRISCVS ADORAT
ORBIS, NEC TE QVI VINCERE POSSIT, ERIT.

The medieval Royal midwife rubbed her lady's belly with oils and unguents in order to hasten birth or deftly used her stiletto-like, specially grown finger nail to break the waters. She would have urged her lady to go up and down stairs for an hour, massaged, stretched and dilated the genital area and birth canal, and, once her patient was sitting in the birthing stool, she would press on the belly to push the child downwards. Birth was usually expected within 20 contractions or '*pangs*'. If it took longer, the '*gossips*' would open and shut drawers, unlock chests and untie knots in the vain hope that this would encourage the womb to bring forth! If the baby was in the breech position, midwives would attempt to turn the child manually. This still happens today but then, unlike now, the practice was a danger in itself. For years it was thought the position of the unborn child would right itself if the labouring mother was rolled around on her bed, shaken vigorously or repeatedly tossed into the air from a blanket — 13-year-old Margaret Beaufort was subjected to these methods as she laboured with the future Henry VII in January 1457.

As for pain relief? There was none. Indeed, it was believed that all women, Royals included, deserved to suffer in childbirth. As was stated in the book of Genesis 3:16 — '*To the woman he said, "I will greatly increase your pain in childbearing; with pain you will give birth to children"*.' Labour pains were thought to be God's way of punishing Eve for taking a bite of the apple in the Garden of Eden. Some Royal ladies wore birth girdles in the belief that these would help relieve labour pangs. Big in the Middle Ages, these belts were religious relics thought to have been worn by the mothers of saints and holy figures. It was believed that by donning such a pious piece of cloth, labour pains would surely be eased. Parish churches hired out whatever birth girdles they happened to have in their possession but England's Queens had access to truly '*top-notch*' ones. The '*Our Lady Girdle*', donated to Westminster Abbey by Edward the Confessor in the 11th century and believed to have been worn by the Virgin Mary herself, was dispatched to Gascony when Eleanor of Provence, Henry III's Queen, gave birth to her daughter Beatrice on June 24 1242. It was worn again in 1303 by Edward I's youngest daughter Elizabeth for the birth of her son, Hugh. And as she labored with the future Henry VIII in late June 1491, Elizabeth of York paid the Benedictine monks of Westminster Abbey 16 shillings (the equivalent of £3500 today) for its hire. Continuing with the religious theme, many Royal mothers-to-be turned to prayer. They were encouraged to call upon the saints for help during childbirth. Thomas of Brotherton (born June 1 1300) the son of Edward I and Marguerite of France, was named after St. Thomas Becket, whose name his mother had cried out during labour and whom she credited with easing her pains. St Margaret, the patron saint of childbirth, was also regularly called upon and several princesses including Margaret, the future Queen of Scotland (born 1240), Margaret Tudor (Henry VIII's elder sister born November 28 1489), and Margaret, ninth child and sixth daughter of Edward I (born September 11 1327) were named for her. In January 1245, the fourth child of Henry III and Eleanor of Provence was named Edmund, after St Edmund whose name she had continually chanted throughout labour. It wasn't unheard of for Royal Ladies, or rather their attendants, to meddle with magic in order to alleviate labour pains. As Mary Queen of Scots gave birth to her only child, James, in June 1566, her attendant, the Countess of Atholl, attempted to cast the pangs of childbirth onto a certain Lady Reres who was also in the throes of labour at the Scottish court. Lady Reres' pains increased - but then so did the Queen's.

Right:
The children of Henry VII, showing Prince Henry (1491 - 1547), Arthur Prince of Wales (1486 - 1502) and Princess Margaret (1489 - 1541), circa 1498

Change started to come in the 17th century with the invention of gynaecological instruments such as forceps. Henrietta Maria, Queen of Charles I, was the first women in the world to give birth with the aid of this then top-secret device. Male doctors, having studied the business of childbirth, began to arrive in the delivery room. There were certainly men — and women — aplenty in the birth chamber when Mary Beatrice of Modena, the second wife of the Catholic James II gave birth in June 1688. Up to 200 by all accounts. The reason for this was that there were rumours that the Queen was not pregnant and it had been planned for another woman's newborn to be sneaked into the room in a warming pan. The crowds were present to witness the birth and ensure that nothing untoward happened. It didn't but rumours still persisted that a changeling child had been smuggled in. The baby prince's Protestant half-sister, Anne, was the chief rumour-monger even though she hadn't been present at the birth. Mary Beatrice, a Catholic like her husband, was upset and confused by her stepdaughter's malicious lies. But Anne and her sister Mary swore it was the truth in order to win the crown away from their father and his son. They succeeded. Within six months, the abdicating King, his wife and baby son had fled to France. As a result of this episode, from then on Royal mothers close to the throne were required to have the births of their babies verified by a Minister of the Crown. It was a custom that continued until well into the 20th century — although the Minister would wait in an adjoining room rather than the birthing chamber itself.

Birth being the dangerous business it was, many a Royal lady — and often also her baby - perished while giving birth or soon afterwards. In 1503, Elizabeth of York, wife of Henry VII, passed away a week after giving birth to her eighth child, a daughter, who did not survive long after her mother. Jane Seymour died less than a fortnight after giving birth to Henry VIII's longed for heir in October 1537 — although the Prince survived. Following Henry's death, his sixth wife Katherine Parr remarried — to Jane Seymour's brother Thomas - but she passed away giving birth to a daughter who only lived for a short while after. Perhaps most tragic death of all, though, was that of Princess Charlotte of Wales, George VI's daughter and heir, in November 1817, aged just 21. Married to Leopold of Saxe Coburg, Charlotte spent her pregnancy quietly but ate heavily and got little exercise. When her medical team began prenatal care in August 1817, they put her on a strict diet, hoping to reduce the size of the child at birth. However, the diet, and occasional bleeding treatments using leeches, seemed to weaken her.

Much of Charlotte's day-to-day care was undertaken by Sir Richard Croft. He was not a physician but an '*accoucheur*', or male midwife, much in fashion among the well-to-do. Croft had calculated a due date of October 19 but Charlotte did not go into labour until November 3. Although she was fully dilated after 24 hours, the labour was protracted and she pushed for hour after hour. Today she would have undergone a C-section but it was not an option in the 1800s — not if the mother was going to survive. Croft had forceps and knew how to use them but he hesitated. Forceps could injure the baby and Croft knew he would be blamed if this was the case. He allowed Charlotte to push for 24 hours — reportedly, for the last six hours, the baby's head was visible. Finally, Charlotte's son was born – dead, having died at some point during the labour. Less than six hours later, Charlotte passed away from a severe haemorrhage, almost certainly due to a protracted labour. This was almost certainly due to the protracted labour. At the loss of Charlotte and her child, the country plunged into a period of mourning that lasted for several weeks.

But what of the Royal babies themselves? Those that survived? The time into which they were born dictated how they were cared for. Although it's rumoured that Anne Boleyn wished to feed the infant Elizabeth herself, Royal mothers did not breast-feed but immediately handed their newborns over to a wet-nurse. The qualities required in a Royal wet-nurse were subject to changing fashions. The ideal Medieval model was a young woman with a pink and white complexion. Red headed wet-nurses were avoided because it was believed that the baby absorbed the characteristics of the woman nursing them — and red headed were thought to have fearsome tempers. Interestingly this changed during the Tudor period, the Tudors being tawny-headed themselves. '*Rosy cheeks, a white skin, thick reddish hair, a thick neck and a hopeful, brave disposition*', were the attributes listed. By Stuart times, the red-headed, freckled wet-nurse had fallen out of favour — it

Left:

Queen Charlotte (1744-1818) cradling the sleeping future King George IV (1762-1830). George IV was King of Great Britain and Ireland between 1820 and 1830

was thought her milk would be sour. A healthy '*brown*' complexion was preferred and stayed in vogue for the next 200 years. Alice de Leygrave, Edward II's wet-nurse in the 1280s, was described as '*the king's mother. . . who suckled him in his youth.*' Anne Launcelyn was appointed wet-nurse to the infant Henry VIII in the 1490s and as a result she was ordered to live chastely and was held responsible for any ill health he suffered. If he had colic, she was purged. If her milk supply was inadequate, she was made to eat stewed udder of goats or sheep, or powdered earthworms — it was thought these '*cures*' would produce more milk. One Christabella Wyndham was wet-nurse to the baby Charles II in the 1630s. But that's not all she was. It was Christabella who introduced Charles to 'that little fantastical man called Cupid,' as she later put it. She seduced Charles when he was 15! Mrs Muttlebury, the wet-nurse of the eldest daughter of George III was carefully vetted before she took up her appointment in autumn 1766. She had to be approved by the head of the nursery, in addition to a doctor and two surgeons. The baby she had been suckling and her elder child were brought in for inspection to show that both thrived. When she was accepted as wet-nurse, Mrs Muttleberry had to devote herself to six months unconditional feeding of the little Princess. She was allowed no visitors, not even her own children, in case they distracted her. She was also ordered to wear silks, brocade and the finest lace to ensure that the Royal baby came into contact with superior fabrics only!

Kings and Queens had little hands-on input into the lives of their offspring. As a three-month-old baby, for instance, the future Elizabeth I was moved to her own '*nursery palace*' at Hatfield — although it was said that her mother, Anne Boleyn, would have preferred to keep her daughter with her. Christenings however were an exception — particularly if the baby was heir to the throne. They were some of the grandest occasions ever seen at court as the Monarch showed off his heir — and his riches.

Henry VI's only son, Edward of Westminster, was christened in Westminster Abbey in October 1453. The font was arranged in russet cloth of gold, surrounded by a blaze of tapers. The christening mantle (robe) cost £500 (hundreds of thousands of pounds today) and was a rich embroidery of pearls and precious stones, lined with fine white linen to insure the brocade and gems didn't come into contact with the baby's delicate skin. Unfortunately Henry himself was unaware of the grandeur of this as he was in a state of mental collapse.

Arthur, the first-born son of Henry VII and Elizabeth of York, arrived a month prematurely so arrangements for his lavish christening were brought forward. The baptism took place at Winchester Cathedral on September 24 1486, the baby having been born in the town four days earlier as Henry VII had wished, believing Winchester to be the site of King Arthur's Camelot. Following the baptism, the christening party proceeded to the shrine of St Swithun, the cathedral's saint, where hymns were sung and '*spices and hypocras, with other sweet wines [in] great plenty*' enjoyed.

Edward VI was christened in the chapel at Hampton Court on October 15 1537 in a lavish midnight ceremony in front of 400 people. This was the first christening of a prince in England for more than a quarter of a century, and every care was taken to make the event as elaborate and impressive as possible. The three-day-old baby was carried under a canopy wearing a richly decorated '*chrisom cloth*' and his wet-nurse and midwife walked alongside the bearers of the train and torchbearers surrounded the canopy. After the Prince had been baptized by the Archbishop of Canterbury, spice, hippocras, bread and sweet wine were served and then the torch-lit procession made its way out of the Chapel back to the Queen's apartments. Christening gifts included a gold cup from the Lady Mary (the prince's half-sister and also godmother), three bowls and two pots of silver and gilt from the Archbishop, and the same from the Duke of Norfolk, and two flagons and two pots of silver and gilt from the Duke of Suffolk.

The three-day Catholic christening of the future James I of England and VI of Scotland took part at Stirling Castle in December 1566 when he was six-months-old. His mother, Mary Queen of Scots, refused to let the Archbishop of St Andrews, whom she referred to as '*a pocky priest*' spit in the child's mouth, as was then the custom. The entertainment culminated in a banquet in the Great Hall. The guests sat at a round table, in imitation of King Arthur and his knights, and the food was brought in on a mobile stage, pulled by members of the court dressed

as satyrs and nymphs. The English guests were offended because they were depicted as satyrs with tails. A child dressed as an angel was lowered in a giant globe from the ceiling and gave a recitation. The banquet ended with a great fireworks display — the first ever witnessed in Scotland. For the baptism of the future Charles II at the Chapel Royal on June 27 1630, the Lord Mayor of London presented a silver font. The four-week-old baby's attendants were awarded the following gifts — a chain of rubies for the wet-nurse, silver plate for the dry-nurse, a selection of silver spoons, cups and salt cellars for the six official cradle rockers. The baby Prince himself received the gift of a jewel from an uncle.

The baptism of Prince George, the month-old, first-born son and heir to King George III, in September 1762, was an occasion for as much splendour as the proud new father could muster. A new gilded mahogany state bed '*of superlative magnificence*' - embellished and ornamented with carvings, white ostrich plumes, gold lace-trimmed crimson velvet valances and curtains, and five mattresses was built for Queen Charlotte to lounge upon during the ceremony. The regal new mother's head rested against a '*white satin pillow bordered with flowers worked in gold and spangles*'.

Left:
Children of King Charles I. Purporting to be by Van Dyke and showing Charles II (1630-1685), James II (1633-1701) and Henrietta (1644-1670) but is a composite picture as Henrietta was 14-years-younger than Charles and not born till after Van Dyke died

'I maintain that a child can never be as well nursed by a lady of rank and nervous and refined temperament - for the less feeling and the more like an animal the wet-nurse is, the better for the child.'

Victorian Royal Babies

It is thanks to the fecundity of Queen Victoria that, by the beginning of the 20th century, much of Europe was ruled by her children and grandchildren. However, her own conception in August 1818, and birth the following May, were fraught with urgency as the middle-aged sons of George III raced each other in an attempt to provide Britain with an heir to the throne - a contest that became known as *'Hymen's War Terrific'*. It was even whispered in some quarters that Edward, Duke of Kent could not be Victoria's father — not when the 51-year-old Duke of Kent had never fathered a child by his French Canadian mistress of 30 years, Julie St Laurent. Yet within a few months of marrying Victoire, the Dowager Princess of Leiningen, in 1818, miraculously the new Duchess of Kent was with child. In April 1819, when she was eight months pregnant, Victoire made a mad dash across Europe in order that their child would be born on British soil and therefore have his or her legitimacy for the throne declared by dignitaries. The strapped-for-cash Duke drove the Phaeton coach himself in order to save money. Following close behind was one Frau Siebold, a female obstetrician who had qualified as a surgeon — a rarity at the time. Fortunately, the good Frau's expertise was not required en-route as the Duchess gave birth once she had safely arrived at Kensington Palace.

'*Plump as a partridge… more of a pocket Hercules than a pocket Venus*', is how the Duke of Kent described his spirited baby daughter when she born on May 24 1819 after a six hour labour. Mother Victoire, meanwhile, broke with convention by insisting on feeding the baby herself. '*I would have been desperate to see my little darling on someone else's breast,*' she wrote to her own mother. '*Everybody was quite astonished.*' It is interesting to speculate that if Victoire hadn't made this unexpected break with precedence and handed her daughter over to a wet-nurse as expected, she may well have fallen pregnant again before the Duke's unexpected death in January 1820. If she had given birth to a son after Victoria, the '*pocket Hercules*' whose name went on to encapsulate an age, would never have ascended the throne.

Victoire was reduced to tears at the christening of her baby daughter at Kensington Palace in June 1819 due to the behaviour of her brother-in-law, the Prince Regent. He only told the baby's parents the date of the christening at the very last minute, dictated what her name should be — Alexandrina Victoria - and insisted that only he, out of the baby's godparents, be present. He also refused to speak to the baby's father, who was his brother, and refused to attend the post-christening dinner afterwards. Baby '*Drina*' as she was known had a lonely, isolated childhood but when she came to the throne as an 18-year-old in 1837,

Right:
Queen Victoria and Prince Albert with five of their children in 1846

she knew her own mind. She insisted on being known as Victoria and, in February 1840, married her German cousin, Prince Albert of Saxe Coburg and Gotha. It was a passionate love match and within weeks, Victoria discovered she was pregnant. She was not happy, pronouncing it '*too dreadful.*' She went on to write to her uncle, King Leopold of Belgium. '*I am really upset about it and it is spoiling my happiness as I have always hated the idea.*' No wonder when, shortly before the birth of this first child in November 1840, her shape was described by her obstetrician, Charles Locock, in less than complementary terms. *'Her figure is now most extraordinary,'* he wrote. *'She goes without stays or anything that keeps her shape within bounds. She is more like a barrel than anything else.'*

Victoria went on to have eight further pregnancies, making nine babies over the space of 17 years. This was a tremendous physical feat, and a dangerous one given the high rates of maternal mortality at the time. She and Albert believed they should lead by example and show themselves as a loving, happy family to their subjects — in direct contrast to Victoria's louche Hanoverian uncles who came before her. However, she never enjoyed being pregnant. '*I think much more of our being like a cow or a dog at such moments. I positively think those ladies who are always "enceinte" quite disgusting,*' she wrote somewhat hypocritically.. '*It is more like a rabbit or guinea-pig than anything else and really it is not very nice.*' Victoria was plagued by depression and volatile mood swings during her pregnancies. She complained of '*aches and sufferings... miseries and plagues,*' and felt '*so pinned down*' it was as if she had had her '*wings clipped*'. She would have terrible quarrels with Albert, following him even when he left the room, 'to have it all out'. Although she hated being pregnant, she was upset when, after the birth of her ninth and final child, Princess Beatrice in 1857, her physician recommended that she should have no more children, for fears for her sanity. Victoria knew this would mean no more sex as Albert regarded it as a reproductive rather than a recreational activity. '*Oh doctor,*' she is reported to have said. '*Does this mean I can have no more fun in bed?*'

It was during the birth of her eighth child, Prince Leopold in April 1853, that Victoria became the unlikely pioneer of pain relief in childbirth. She employed the services of Dr John Snow, a Yorkshire farmer's son who had used chloroform as anaesthetic. Her senior physician had grave doubts, not least because of Dr Snow's humble origins, but Victoria overruled him. She found, '*Oh that blessed chloroform. . .soothing and delightful beyond measure*' and insisted Dr Snow again be in attendance when she gave birth to Princess Beatrice four years later. Victoria's decision was not universally approved. Protests were staged on religious and medical grounds but the procedure gained popularity and became known as the '*Anaesthesia de la Reine*'. Victoria advised all her female descendents to give birth while under the influence of the '*soothing*' and '*delightful*' drug. Her beloved Albert was by her side during each of her nine labours. '*There could be no kinder, wiser nor more judicious nurse,*' she wrote.

Believing she was a descendent of King David, Victoria sanctioned the circumcision of her four baby sons — Albert Edward, the future Edward VI, born in November 1841, Alfred born August 1844, Arthur born May 1850, and Leopold. Unlike her mother, she was vehemently against breastfeeding her babies. she thought it a disgusting practise. '*The horrors about that peculiarly indelicate nursing - which is far worse than all the other parts,*' she wrote. '*When one is high-born - one can avoid and ought to avoid. I maintain that a child can never be as well nursed by a lady of rank and nervous and refined temperament - for the less feeling and the more like an animal the wet-nurse is, the better for the child.*' In Victoria's view, the perfect wet-nurse was '*very dark and thin and with plenty of milk.*' The Queen was a strict employee — the wet-nurse of first born Vicky had to stand while feeding her charge as sitting was forbidden. The wet-nurse she employed for her first-born son, the future Edward VII, turned out to be a murderess! In 1855, following a quarrel with her husband, the woman slit the throats of her own six children before trying to kill herself. She was detained at a home for the mentally insane for the rest of her life.

Victoria found her offspring particularly unappealing when they were babies. '*Abstractedly, I have no tender feeling for them till they have become a little human,*' she wrote. '*An ugly baby is a very nasty object — and the prettiest is frightful when undressed until about four months - . . . in short as long as they have their big body and little limbs and that terrible froglike action. I like them better than I did, if they are nice and pretty.*' However, she could also be a doting mother. Victoria's diary entries in the 1840s and 50s, reveal a mother who delighted in her children. '*It seems like a dream having a child,*' she wrote after Vicky's birth and she delighted in showing the little Princess off to her ladies-in-waiting, writing, '*She was awake and very sweet and I must say, I was very proud of her.*' Within a year, son and heir, Prince

Left:
Queen Victoria and her two elder children

Above Right:
'The Royal Mother', by unknown artist

Albert Edward had been born with his proud mama noting, '*Our little boy is a wonderfully strong and large child.*' Of Princess Alice, born in April 1843, she wrote, '*She is a pretty and large baby, whom I am really proud of, and we think she will be la Beaute of the family...*'

Victoria put on lavish christenings for her first two babies. Princess Vicky christened on her parents' first wedding anniversary on February 10 1841, wore a specially commissioned gown, made from the same fabrics as her mother's wedding dress — Spitalfields silk satin and Honiton lace. The baby '*looked very dear in a white Honiton point lace robe and mantle, over white satin,*' wrote the Queen. This became the famous British christening gown which, after this first wearing, was worn by more than 60 royal babies before it was '*retired*' due to its deteriorating condition in 2004. An exact replica was made by Queen Elizabeth II's dressmaker, Angela Kelly, to replace it.

For the christening of Prince Albert Edward in January 1842 at St George's Chapel, Windsor, Queen Victoria, spent thousands of pounds creating an event of '*unprecedented grandeur*'. Two royal baptismal fonts were used — the 1630 font, which was re-gilt and ornamented for the occasion, was used in conjunction with the new Lily Font. The christening celebrations included a banquet, fireworks and other entertainments and a christening cake '*on a scale of magnitude and magnificence quite unrivalled, [it] stands on a silver plateau about 30 inches in diameter, and is, with its figured ornaments, upwards of 4 feet high. Without its ornaments it would appear like a Coliseum of sugar*'.

Below:
The Christening of Victoria, Princess Royal, 10 February 1841

Below Right:
The Christening of The Prince of Wales, 25 January 1842

The Queen wore state jewels, the women wore evening dresses and tiaras, and the men wore uniforms and decorations.

In a reversal of the typical roles of the time, Victoria devoted herself to regal duties while Albert took responsibility for the upbringing of the children. He had a hands-on approach to child rearing and Lady Lyttleton, a governess, remembered seeing him playing with Vicky, who he especially adored — '*Albert tossed and romped with her, making her laugh and crow and kick heartily*'. Victoria, by contrast, was distant and guarded. She looked on as Albert took control of all aspects of the children's development. At first Albert found this task fulfilling and stimulating, appealing to his sense of himself as an expert in human behaviour. '*There is certainly a great charm, as well as deep interest, in watching the development of feelings and faculties in a little child,*' he once remarked. He criticised his wife for her lack of interest, *'It is a pity you find no consolation in the company of your children. The trouble lies in the mistaken notion the function of a mother is to be always correcting, scolding and ordering them about',* he wrote in a letter to her. But as a father Albert expected way beyond what the majority of his children were capable of. Child genius Princess Vicky may have thrived in this hot-house environment but according to Baron Stockmar, Albert's advisor, the regime would give any child brain fever.

The plan began when the children were infants, with the instilling of discipline. '*The chief objects here,*' Albert described, '*are their physical development, the actual rearing up, the training to obedience.*' The children frequently received '*a real punishment by whipping*' if they misbehaved and Albert himself would hit his children's fingers during piano lessons when they played the wrong notes. When the children turned out to be just children rather than the paragons of virtue and intellect he had hoped for, Albert suspected that it was a result of their reprobate Stuart and Hanoverian inheritance. It could not possibly have come from him.

With Albert's untimely death in 1861 when Beatrice, his and Victoria's youngest child, was only four, the practise of trying to make the Royal children perfect died too. Victoria, as is well known, was poleaxed by grief for many years. However, in a rare moment of honest introspection she was later to comment — '*You will find as your children grow up that as a rule your children are a bitter disappointment — their greatest object being to do precisely what their parents do not wish and have anxiously tried to prevent. Often when children have been less watched and less taken care of — the better they turn out! This is inexplicable and very annoying!*'.

Considering Victoria had disliked the whole business of being pregnant, giving birth and caring for new-borns, she was obsessive when it came to her pregnant daughters and daughters-in-law. When Princess Alice, the third child of Queen Victoria and Prince Albert, and the great grandmother of the current Duke of Edinburgh, gave birth to her first child in April 1863, Victoria insisted on being present. For the Queen, it was a case of déjà vu as Alice gave birth in the same bed and room she herself had laboured in, and also wore the same night shift Victoria had worn for each of her nine confinements. '*It seemed a strange dream and as if it must be me and dearest Papa — instead of Alice and Louis (Alice's husband, Louis of Hesse).*' Victoria would try to insist on being present when a grandchild was born but that wasn't possible when the first child of the future King Edward VII and Queen Alexandra — and the third in line to the throne - was born in early 1864. although, at seven-months-pregnant, Alix had been advised to stay indoors and rest, she was determined to watch husband, Bertie, play ice-hockey on the frozen Virginia Water in Surrey on January 8 of that year. As Bertie played, Alix was whirled around the ice on a chair fitted with runners. Her pains started after luncheon and she wished to return to Frogmore House where they were staying. Bertie, however, pooh-poohed the idea and finished his game. By the time they got back to Frogmore, Alix was in labour proper. Her lady-in-waiting, Lady Macclesfield, was forced to send for the local doctor as the six doctors who had been booked to deliver the baby, due in March, were obviously not in attendance. As it turned out, the local doctor didn't arrive in time and, just before 9pm, Lady Mac, as she was known, delivered the tiny baby onto her own red flannel petticoat which she'd removed for the purpose. While Prince Albert Victor (known in the family as Eddy) genuinely was premature, Alexandra pretended her subsequent five babies were, too, in order to stop Queen Victoria from interfering and being present at their births. But Alexandra was a very different kind of Royal mother to Victoria. She was regarded as exceptional because she visited her children's nursery every morning and evening, and often bathed her babies herself — '*She was in her glory when she could run up to the nursery, put on a flannel apron, wash the children herself and see them asleep in their little beds*'

Left:
Prince Albert, Queen Victoria and their nine children in 1857

Victoria was appalled when daughters Vicky and Alice chose to breast feed their own babies — although Vicky did not feed her first three children herself. Queen Victoria not only disapproved of Vicky nursing her younger babies but was furious at her for influencing younger sister Alice to nurse her newborn as well. The Queen had thought that Alice, like herself, '*disliked the disgusting details of the nursery...all and every one of which Vicky delights in*', and was pained to discover otherwise. '*There is in everything the animal side of our nature but it hurts me deeply that my own two daughters should set at defiance the advice of a Mother of 9 children, 46 years old. It does make my hair stand on end to think that my two daughters should turn into cows.*'

Victoria duly named cows in the Royal dairy after her two 'animal-like' daughters.

Queen Victoria's comment on seeing her great grandson and heir, Prince Edward, the future Edward VIII and Duke of Windsor, for the first time.

'A pretty child – a fine, strong boy'

Victoria's Great Grandchildren

At 10 o'clock in the evening of June 23 1894, at White Lodge in Richmond Park, Princess May, Duchess of York, gave birth to her first child — a little Prince who instantly became third in line to the throne behind his father, Prince George, Duke of York, and grandfather, the Prince of Wales. It hadn't been the easiest of pregnancies, not least because there was '*all sorts of fuss and precautions of all kinds and sorts*' which the very private mother-to-be did not enjoy. Neither did she embrace the changes to her body and described the business of being with child as '*the penalty of being a woman.*' While May was in labour, George bided his time in the library at the Lodge pretending to read '*Pilgrim's Progress*'. '*At 10 a sweet little boy,* 'the Duke wrote in his diary, having seen his new born for the first time. His grandfather the Prince of Wales was at a ball in Windsor that evening and on hearing the happy news, stopped the orchestra so he could announce the birth and raise a glass to the baby Prince. Four days after his birth, his great grandmother Queen Victoria came to visit, declaring that her heir was '*a pretty child — a very fine, strong boy.*' She wrote to her eldest daughter, The Empress Frederick, in Germany, '*You rejoice as I do, indeed, and as the whole nation does, to the most wonderful degree, at the birth of dear Georgie's boy. It is a great pleasure and satisfaction. . .it is true that it has never happened in this country that there should be three direct heirs as well as the sovereign alive.*'

The Duke and Duchess wished to call their son Edward, in memory of George's elder brother, known as '*Eddy*' who had died two years before. But Victoria wanted him to be named after her beloved Albert, the baby's great grandfather. Finally, a compromise was reached. He would be given the names Edward Albert — with the additions of Christian (after his godfather, the King of Denmark), George (after his father and St George, patron saint of England), Andrew (after the patron saint of Scotland), Patrick (Ireland) and David (Wales). Within the family he would always been known as David. At his christening in the Green Drawing Room of White Lodge on 16 July 1894, conducted by Edward White Benson, Archbishop of Canterbury, were his 12 godparents - two Kings, three Queens, two Princes, one Princess, one Duchess, two Dukes and one Grand Duke.

Joy might have been unconfined at the arrival of this new heir to the throne but Princess May was not a natural mother. She didn't wish to breast feed, couldn't abide the noise of a crying baby and indeed found the whole business of child rearing alien. So, it was with a certain amount of relief that she handed her new-born over the newly employed nanny, Mary Peters. At 27, Peters, who was an orphan, was utterly devoted to her charge. Too devoted as it was to turn out.

Right:
The Princess of Wales with her family at Abergeldie Castle, Aberdeenshire. The children are (top, left to right) Princess Mary, Prince Edward; (bottom, left to right) Prince Henry, Prince George, Prince John and Prince Albert

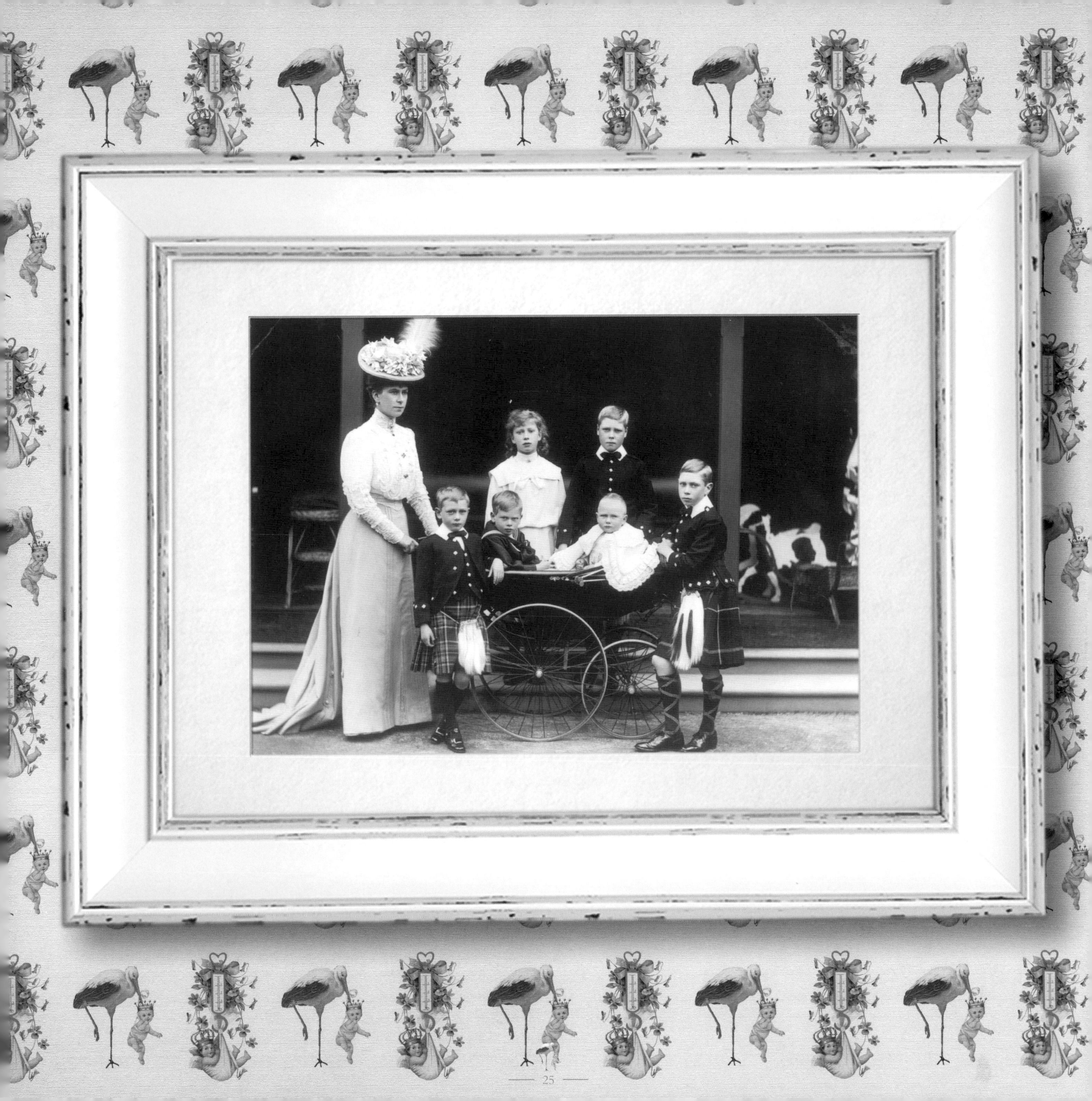

May produced another son at 3.30am on December 14 1895 - an unfortunate date as it had been on this day 34 years before that Prince Albert passed away. '*Grandmama was rather distressed,*' said the Prince of Wales but, ever the diplomat, he recommended that Prince George ask Victoria to be this baby's godmother and that he should also be named Albert. Victoria was delighted. '*It is a great pleasure to me that he is to be called Albert,*' she commented, '*but, in fact, he could hardly have been called by any other name. I am all impatience to see the new one, born on such a sad day but rather more dear to me, especially as he will be called by that dear name which is a byword for all that is great and good.*' The baby was christened Albert Frederick Arthur George three months later at St Mary Magdelene's church, Sandringham. At 18-months old, big brother David behaved impeccably at the ceremony until his baby brother started to yell. Edward decided to yell louder and was promptly removed. Albert was always known within the family as Bertie.

As she had with David, May handed Bertie over to Nanny Peters as soon as she possibly could. May would see her boys perhaps twice a day when they were brought to her. She never ventured up to the nursery — and this turned out to be a grave mistake with repercussions affecting both David and Bertie into adulthood. Mary Peters was not a well woman. She was pathologically protective towards David with the result that no one else in the nursery dare touch him, talk to him or do anything for him in case she either turned on them or the boy himself. To make matters worse she paid little attention to Bertie, underfeeding and neglecting him because David was her sole concern. When she took David to see

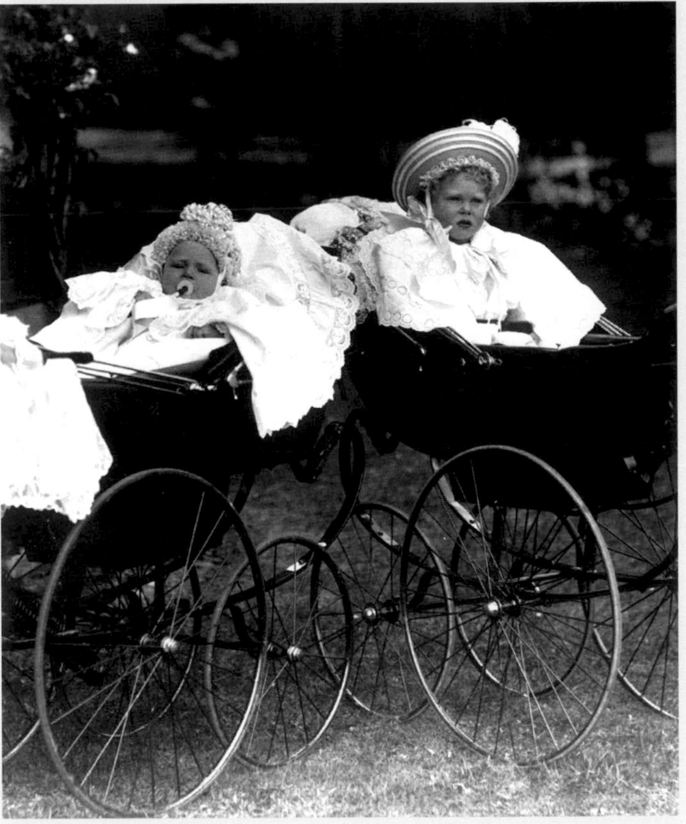

Left:
The future King Edward VIII's christening day, 16 July 1894. Queen Victoria, her son 'Bertie' who became Edward VII, grandson Georgie who became George V, and great grandson David who became King Edward VIIII

Above Right:
Edward Albert Windsor,1895

Below Right:
Prince Albert and Prince Edward

Left:
Baby Albert, 1896

Right:
From left, new born Princess Mary, Prince Edward and Prince Albert

his parents every night before bed, she would twist and pinch his arms just before going into the room. Therefore, he would be crying when they saw him and they would order her to remove him immediately. With regards to Bertie, she would give him his bottle while out on walks in his unsprung perambulator which resulted in him suffering from severe wind. Then when he started eating soft solids, she would snatch his food away before he had barely had chance to eat anything. This treatment laid the foundation of the gastric problems he was to suffer for all his life.

When May became pregnant for a third time in autumn 1896, a young London-born nursery nurse called Charlotte or '*Lala*' Bill was taken on as second nanny. It was Lala who discovered that David was covered with bruises and that timid, nervous little Bertie was being neglected. Lala decided she had to do something, plucked up her courage and confided in one of Princess May's ladies who went on to reveal the truth to May herself. Peters was fired the same day, although, at first, she refused to go. Within a week, she had been admitted to hospital with a nervous breakdown and never recovered. Lala took over. In addition to Bertie's gastric problems as the result of Peters' treatment, it is possible that David's future relationships with women were affected by the abuse he received as a very small boy. Almost as shocking as the maltreatment itself is the fact that neither George nor May had suspected anything was amiss. Like May, George's parental instincts were sadly lacking. He had no patience with the boys, didn't know how to speak to them and was often heard demanding that Lala Bill, '*Stop that child from crying.*'

Princess Victoria Alexandra Alice Mary was born on April 27 1897. She was always to be known as Mary although her great grandmother Queen Victoria wanted the baby christened '*Diamond*' as this was the year of her Diamond Jubilee. The baby's parents politely refused so Her Majesty had to be satisfied with calling Mary "my little Diamond Jubilee baby". Her baptism took place at St Mary Magdalene's Church on June 7 1897 and conducted by William Dalrymple Maclagan, Archbishop of York. Her godparents included her great grandmother Queen Victoria and the Prince and Princess of Wales who were also her grandparents. The Yorks' now had a daughter but May, although pleased with her little girl, was as hands-off as she had been with the boys. The little Princess was dispatched to the nursery forthwith. Three years were to pass before May and George added to their family. In that time, the relationship between parents and offspring became no closer, although George admittedly had a soft spot for his daughter. The three siblings, however, formed a close bond. Lively David was the leader, Mary was a tomboy while middle child Bertie remained the shy one who was often over-looked. After visiting the three children in 1898, Queen Victoria noted that '*David is a delightful child, so intelligent, nice and friendly. The baby is a sweet little thing.*' There was no mention of poor Bertie.

Below:
Princess Royal, Victoria Alexandra Alice Mary in 1898

Right:
Queen Victoria at Osborne with the children of the Duke and Duchess of York (left to right) Prince Albert, Princess Victoria, Prince Edward and Prince Henry on Queen Victoria's lap

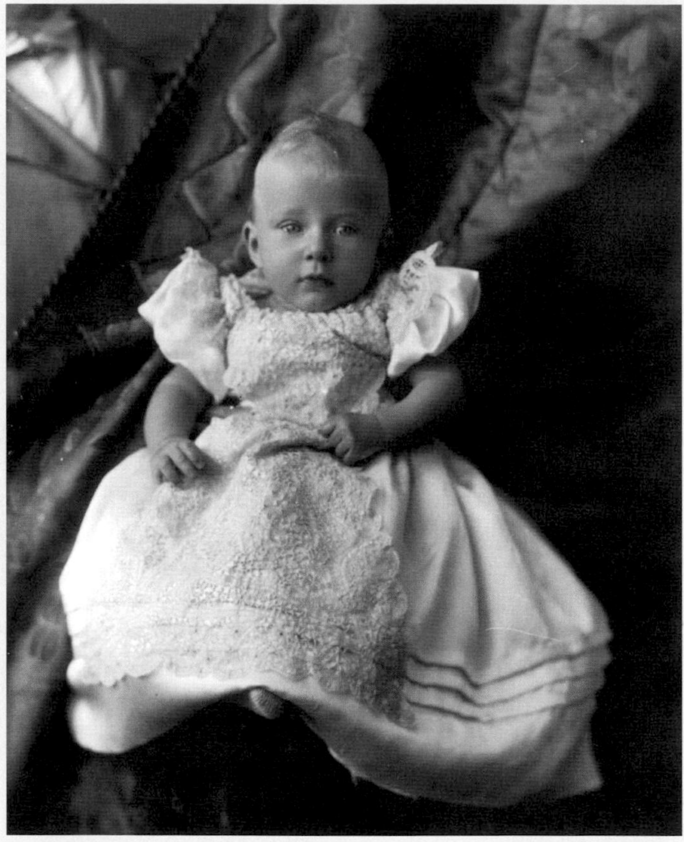

On March 31 1900, May gave birth to another boy. He was named Henry William Frederick Albert but known as Harry - just like as great, great nephew would be 84 years on. He was baptised in the private chapel of Windsor Castle on 17 May 1900, by Randall Thomas Davidson, Bishop of Winchester, and his godparents included Queen Victoria and the German Emperor. '*I think I have done my duty now and may stop,*' May wrote to an aunt. '*Having babies is highly distasteful to me though once they are there they are nice. The children are so pleased with the baby who they think flew in at my window and had to have his wings cut off.*' It's believed six-year-old David suffered from nightmares as the result of this explanation. One of the last photos ever taken of Queen Victoria show her outside Osbourne House on the Isle of Wight, with baby Harry on her knee. The other three York children are standing next to her. At 81, the Queen, now infirm, was deeply worried about dropping her latest great grandson so Lala Bill hid behind the chair and supported the monarch's arm.

George had little to do with the children, believing them to be their mother's concern, after the nanny's, of course. They were frightened of their father and preferred being with their mother — when she deigned to spend time with them, that is. But even when they very small she tended to treat them like adults and seemed surprised when they acted like children. When he was just two, she noted that David had been '*most civil to me*'. The people they really liked being with were their indulgent paternal grandparents, the Prince and Princess of Wales, and in March 1901, following the death of Queen Victoria, the four York children went to stay with the new King Edward and Queen Alexandra while their parents were away touring the colonies. They had indulged their own children and now delighted in doing the same to their '*Georgie pets*', as Granny Alix called them. The King encouraged them to race slices of buttered toast down his trousers, taking bets on who would win, while Alexandra would often cancel the elder children's school lessons so that she could play with them or amuse them. When George and May returned, 18- month-old Harry didn't recognise his parents and cried when his mother lifted him up. In their absence, he had learned to both walk and talk. Four-year-old Mary hid behind her grandmother's skirts although both Bertie and David stepped forward for hugs from their mother. Shortly afterwards, it was decided that these two elder boys leave the nursery and Lala Bill. They were only seven and five-years-old but their parents felt it was time for some '*character building*' so former nursery footman Frederick Finch would now take care of them. Luckily for them, he turned out to be a trusted confidante rather than a tyrant. Their father, meanwhile, decreed that both boys only ever dress in sailor suits or kilts.

At the time of their grandfather's Coronation in August 1902, May, now Princess of Wales, was expecting again. But although she was

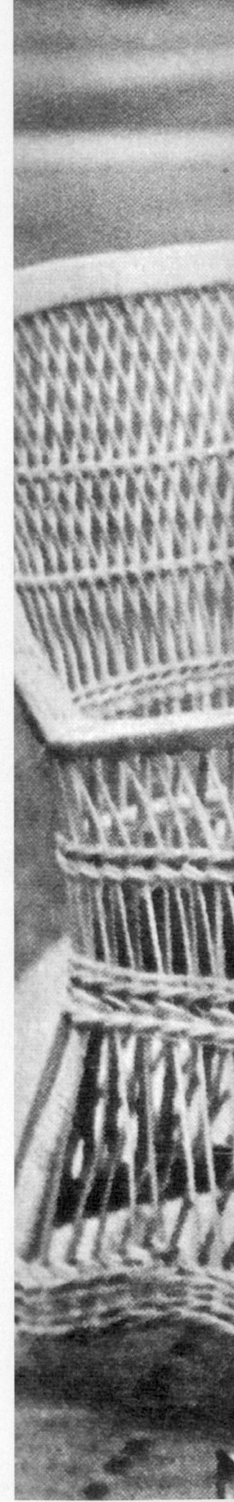

five months pregnant no one would have known. At the Coronation ceremony her corset was as tightly laced as ever, disguising and '*nipping in*' her baby bump. On December 20, Prince George Edward Alexander was born. His father declared, '*I shall soon have a regiment.*' George was christened in the Private Chapel at Windsor Castle on 26 January 1903. In time honoured fashion, little Georgie, as he was known, joined his elder sister and brother in the nursery. Like all well-to-do babies of the time, Georgie wore long dresses trimmed with lace, perhaps with smocking and ribbons, and an elaborate bonnet when in public. The grandest dresses might be over a metre long, with lace decoration. Once the child began to crawl a shorter version was used - this was known as '*short coating*'. Little boys didn't graduate into sailor suits and the like until they were four or five-years-old.

May and George's sixth and final child was born at York Cottage on the Sandringham Estate on July 12 1905. As usual, pregnancy bored May and she felt hemmed in, especially as the seclusion required once she started to '*show*' meant that she was unable to attend the functions and social occasions she enjoyed. Her labour was long and difficult, resulting in Prince John Charles Francis, named after a second brother of George's who had lived for only a day. While May quickly recovered, the tiny Prince, known as Johnnie, had breathing difficulties but was well enough to be christened at the Church of St Mary Magdelene on August 3. His godparents included King Carlos I of Portugal, The Duke of Fife and Princess Alexander of Teck.

Though a '*large and handsome*' baby, by his fourth birthday John had become '*winsome*' and '*painfully slow*'. That same year he suffered his first epileptic seizure and showed signs of a disability, most probably autism. Although Johnnie lived at home, his seizures worsened as the years went by and in 1916 he was sent to live at a small cottage at Sandringham, with his nanny, the ever faithful Lala Bill. In January 1919, aged 13, John suffered a severe seizure and died in his sleep at Wood Farm, with Lala holding his hand. Queen Mary wrote in her diary that it was '*a great shock, tho' for the little boy's restless soul death came as a great relief. Little Johnnie looked very peaceful*'. Lala Bill was devastated and remained devoted to the memory of the young Prince right up to her own death in the 1960s when she was approaching her 90s. On a visit to her house, David, then Duke of Windsor, noticed that the first object he saw when he walked into Lala's house was a large photo of Johnnie as a toddler on her fireplace mantel.

Right:

A royal family group during a visit to Abergeldie, circa 1906. From back, left: Mary, the Princess of Wales holding Prince John, Prince George, Prince Edward, and Prince Albert, seated is Prince Henry

Another notable great grandchild of Queen Victoria includes Lord Louis Francis Albert Victor Nicholas Mountbatten, uncle of the Duke of Edinburgh. A few minutes before his baptism on July 17 1900 at Frogmore House on the Windsor Castle estate, the month-old-baby accidentally knocked off the spectacles of this great grandmother who also happened to be his godmother. It's not known whether she was amused but she certainly managed to keep her cool on an extremely hot summer's day. She'd ordered that a bucket of ice be placed beneath under her chair. Louis was known within the family as '*Dickie*'. Richard wasn't one of Louis Mountbatten's six names so how come he answered to this derivative? It's thanks to Tsar Nicholas II who came on a visit to Britain in 1909. Until this point little Prince Louis was known as Nicky (the shortened version of his fifth name Nicholas) but so was the Tsar. To avoid confusion, Tsar Nicky started calling little Nicky, Dickie. It stuck and from then on, little Nicky was forever known as Dickie!

Victoria was also the great grandmother of the future King Olav V of Norway, future Carol II of Romania, future King Paul and George II of Greece, the future Queen Louise of Sweden and the four Grand Duchesses and the Tsarevich of Russia, the children of the last Tsar and Tsarina, who were executed at Ekaterinburg in 1916.

She had upwards of 80 great grandchildren in all.

The Duke of York on the day of his elder daughter, Elizabeth's, birth.

'We always wanted a child to make our happiness complete'

Elizabeth and Margaret

Elizabeth

Born 21 April 1926, Queen Elizabeth II is the first British Monarch ever to have been born in a private house rather than Royal Castle, Palace or Mansion. With building works ongoing at the Grosvenor Square mansion rented by her parents, the Duke and Duchess of York, the future George VI and Queen Elizabeth, the mother-to-be preferred to give birth at the Mayfair home of her parents rather than labour at her in-laws' Palace. It wasn't an easy birth. The baby was breech and the Duchess was in labour for the best part of a day before doctors deemed that that '*certain line of treatment*'- ie, a Caesarian section - was necessary in the early hours of April 21 1926. The baby girl was born at 2.40am. She was third in line to the throne after her father and Uncle David but there was never any thought that she would one day ascend the throne. Surely her Uncle would marry and have children of his own. Even if he did not, it was presumed that Bertie and Elizabeth would have a son in due course who would take precedence over their daughter. As it was, baby York was the apple of her parents' eye. She was extra special because the Duchess had previously suffered a miscarriage and feared she may never have children as a result. '*You don't know what a tremendous joy it is to Elizabeth and me to have our little girl. We always wanted a child to make our happiness complete and now that it has at last happened, it seems so wonderful and strange,*' Bertie wrote to his mother on the day of his daughter's birth. Queen Mary was equally smitten, far more so than she ever was with her own children. '*The baby is a little darling,*' she wrote, '*with a lovely complexion and pretty fair hair.*'

Christened in the Buckingham Palace private chapel, which would be destroyed by a World War Two bomb some years later, the baby was christened Elizabeth after her mother, Alexandra after her great grandmother who had died the previous year, and Mary after her grandmother. Her grandfather George V approved the choices. The gold, lily-shaped font was transported from Windsor castle and the little Princess was dressed in the heavy satin and Honiton lace gown that had been made for Queen Victoria's eldest child. Her godparents included Prince Arthur, Duke of Connaught, Victoria and Albert's only surviving son, the King and Queen, and her maternal grandmother, Lady Strathmore. Baby Elizabeth apparently cried so much at her christening that '*her nurse dosed her with dill water*', a remedy containing alcohol back in the 1920s — much to the amusement of her uncle, the Prince of Wales.

The Duchess of York adored her baby daughter but lost no time in employing her own childhood nanny to take charge. The strict-but-fair Hertfordshire-born Clara Knight had tended to both the Duchess and her younger brother David, and had most recently cared for the children of Lady Elphinstone, Elizabeth and David's elder sister. This practice of passing-down-the-nanny was very common amongst the British upper classes, had been for years and would be for many more

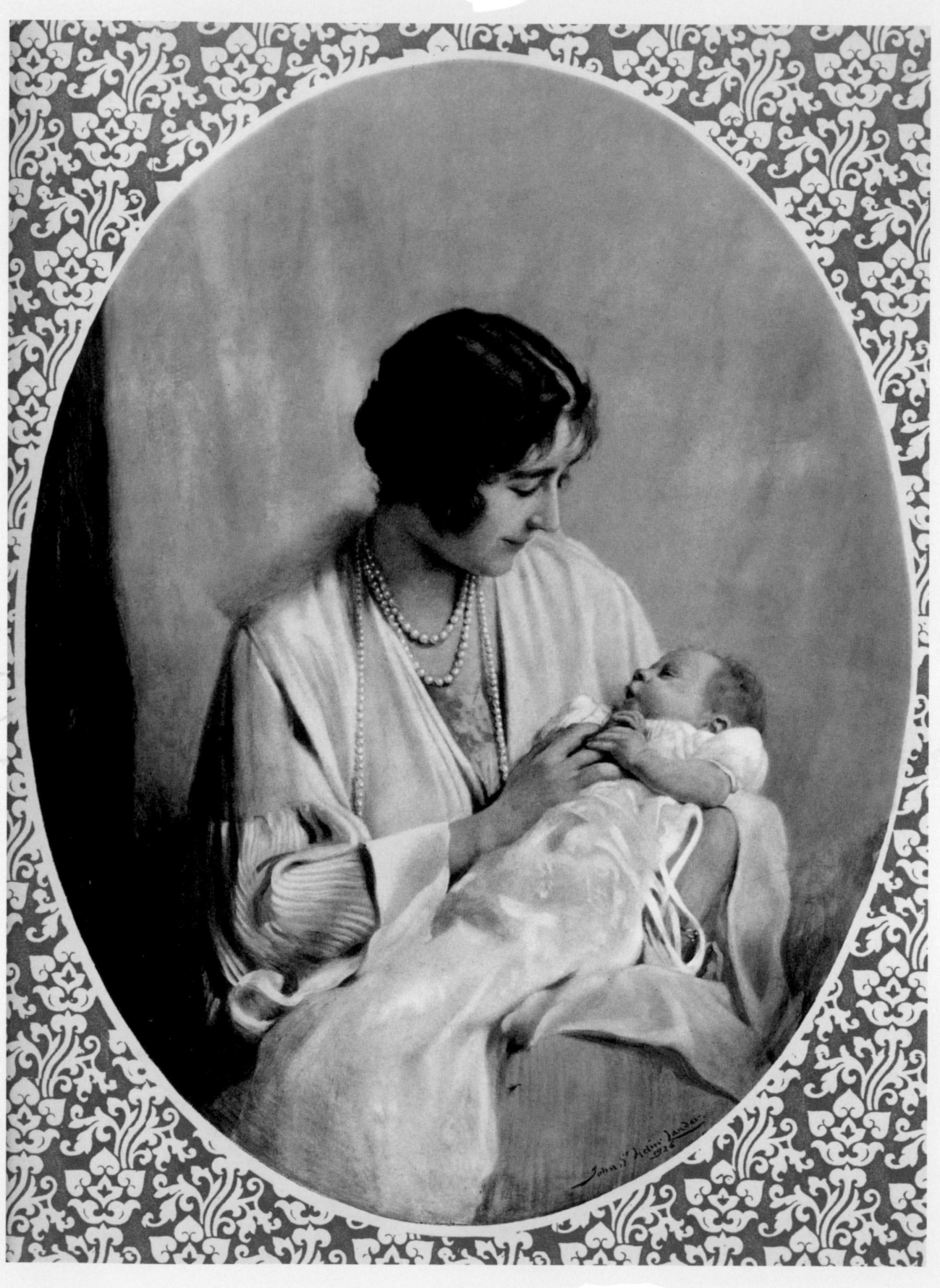

Left:
Portrait of Elizabeth II as a baby held by her mother, Elizabeth. After the painting by John Helier Lander

Below Right:
The Duke and Duchess of York with their baby daughter after her christening in the private chapel at Buckingham Palace, where she received the names Elizabeth Alexandra Mary

to come. Known as '*Alah*' — her young charges could never get their tongues around '*Clara*' — she ruled the nursery, the nursery footmen and assistants. Her word was law. The Duchess gave her complete control with the result that baby Elizabeth - who was always dressed in hand-stitched garments of white cotton - was raised in the same time-honoured way her mother had been. Alah believed in neither pandering to nor pampering children. She and Elizabeth lived in a suite of '*sunny*' rooms at the top of Yorks' house in Mayfair, London, consisting of a day nursery, a night nursery and a bathroom linked by a landing, with wide windows looking down on the park. It was a loving and calm yet neat and ordered environment, and discipline was the order of the day. A strict routine was adhered to at all times with set periods set aside for feeding, bathing, playing, perambulator walks and parental visits. Alah's nursery assistant, was one Margaret McDonald whom Elizabeth named '*Bobo*' and who became the future Queen's dresser and most trusted companion until her death at the age of 89 in 1993.

Queen Mary and King George were doting grandparents to the '*Bambino*', as the Queen called her. Mary would often send a car to fetch baby Elizabeth at teatime and '*the Bambino*' would be shown off to the Queen's guests with Mary herself describing the child as a 'white fluff of thistledown' who had '*the sweetest air of complete serenity*'. When Elizabeth was nine-months-old, at her grandmother's suggestion, her parents were sent on an official tour of Australia and New Zealand — a trip undertaken by sea that would take them away from their baby daughter for six months. But rather than being chastised by the public for leaving her not-yet-one-year-old, the Duchess was applauded for doing her Royal and wifely duty. She was however upset at the prospect of leaving little Elizabeth for so long.

'*Feeling very miserable at leaving the baby,*' she wrote on the morning of departure. '*Went up and played with her and she was so sweet, playing with the buttons on Bertie's jacket quite broke me up. Luckily she doesn't realize anything.*' Having left the nursery, the Duchess '*drank some champagne and tried not to weep*'. Baby Elizabeth was left in the care of her grandparents, the King and Queen, who

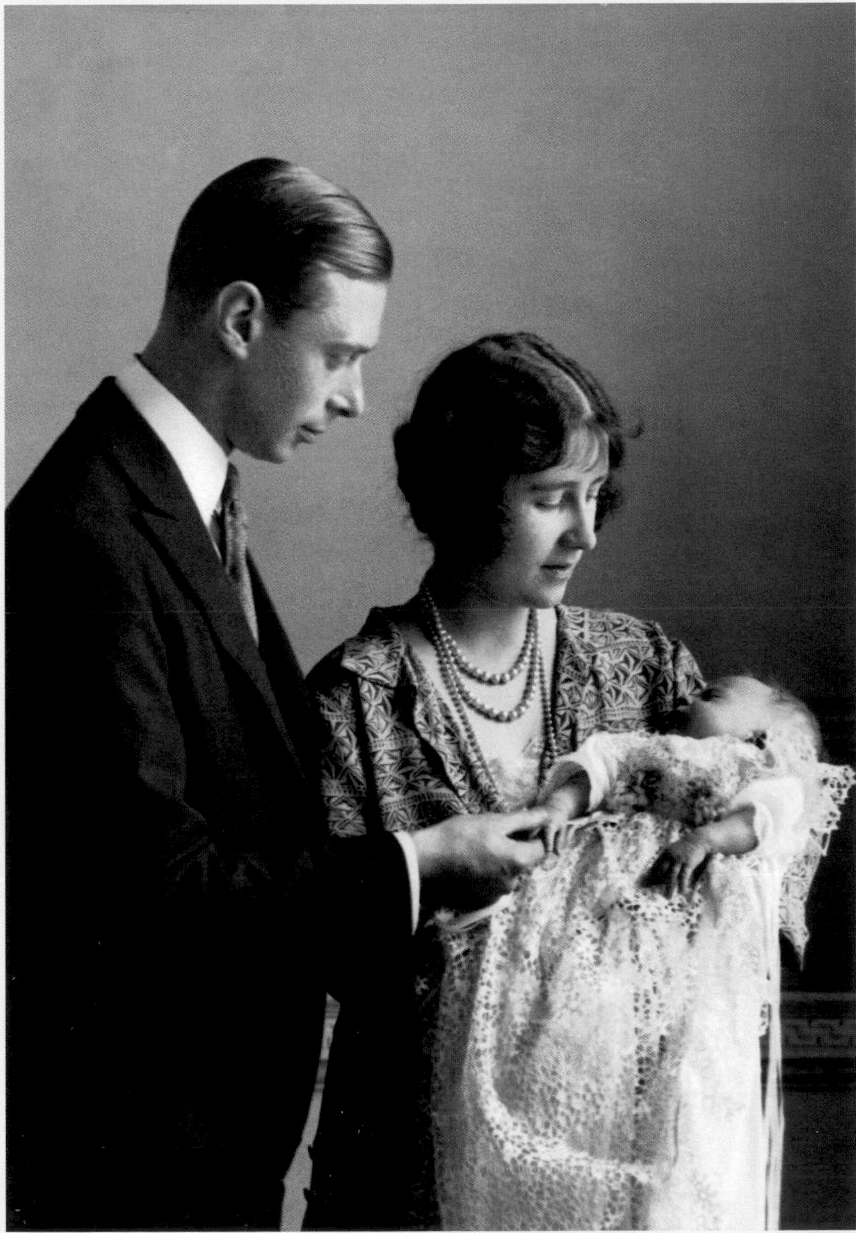

Below:
The Duchess of York with her newborn daughter Princess Elizabeth

Right:
Princess Elizabeth aged two

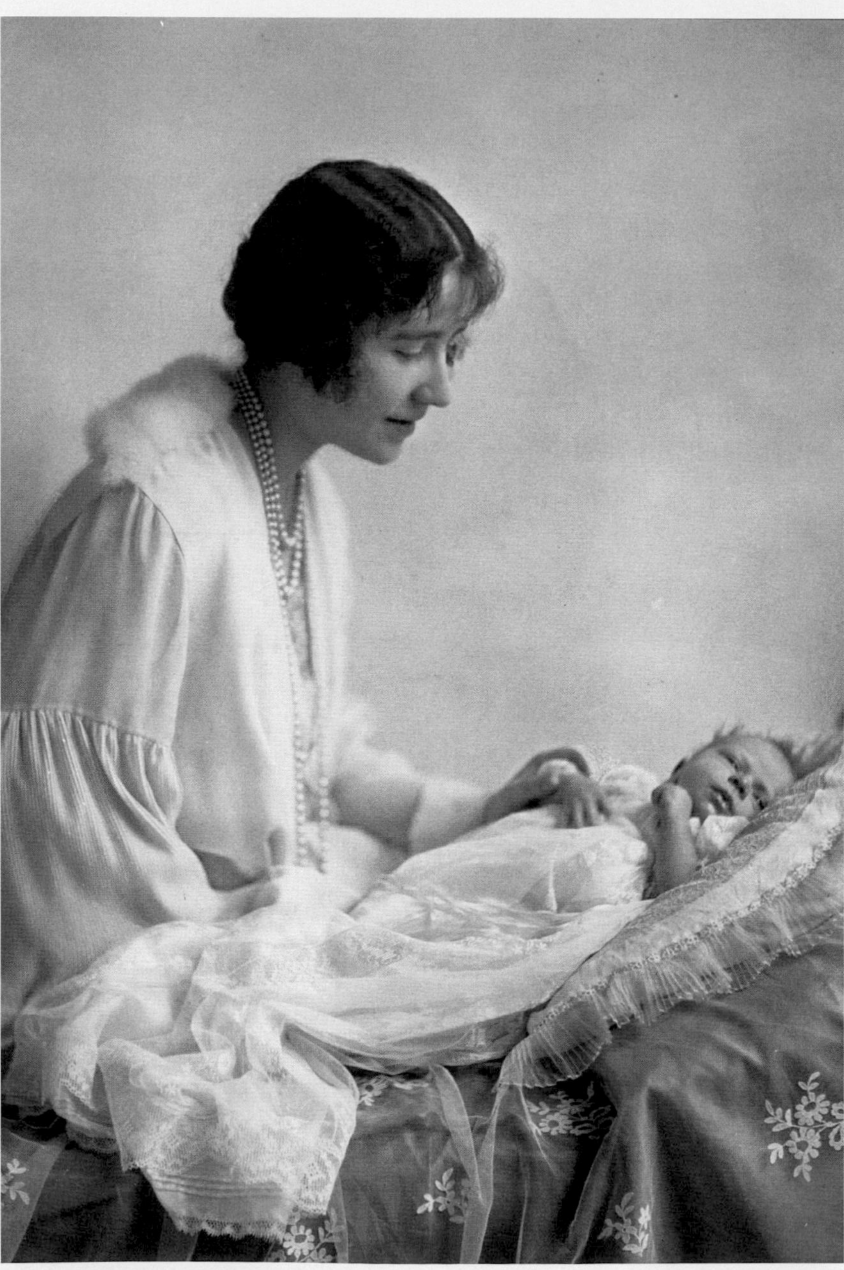

surprisingly turned out to be, in their own way, almost as doting as Edward VII and Alexandra had been with their grandchildren. Mary would see her grand daughter at least three times a day and it was Mary who held her when she made her first balcony appearance when she was a year-old. Meanwhile George V who had never allowed his own children to speak to him unless he addressed them first, was happy to have 'Lilibet', as she called herself, clamber onto his lap and pull his beard. She was without doubt his favourite grandchild. He always requested that she be seated next to him at meal times, would take her to see his horses when at Sandringham and bought her a Shetland pony, Peggy, for her fourth birthday.

It was of course Alah who really took care of Elizabeth while her parents were away. While they were home, too, for that matter. Alah patiently taught the little girl to enunciate the word '*Mummy*'. Since, however, there was nobody to whom the word could be accurately applied, Elizabeth greeted everybody she came across, including family portraits, with the salutation '*Mummy, Mummy!*' When mummy and daddy finally returned to Britain after half a year away, 15-month-old Elizabeth did not recognize them. The little girl burst into tears and refused to go into her mother's arms, clinging to Nanny's skirt before she could be persuaded to join the Royal Family on the balcony of Buckingham Palace. Princess Elizabeth was on her way to becoming a mini superstar. Aged just two-and-a-half, Winston Churchill declared on meeting her for the first time that, '*she is a character. She has an air of authority and reflectiveness that is astonishing in an infant*'. By the time she was three, she was on the cover of '*Time*' magazine, dressed in her trademark yellow rather than the traditional pink for a girl. This set a trend for little girls — and boys — the world over. There was tangible disappointment when the Duchess of York arrived on an official visit to Edinburgh without her daughter. '*I fear it has been a very great disappointment to our people,*' she wrote to Queen Mary. '*It almost frightens me that people love her so much. I suppose that it is a good thing, and I hope that she will be worthy of it, poor little darling.*'

Left:

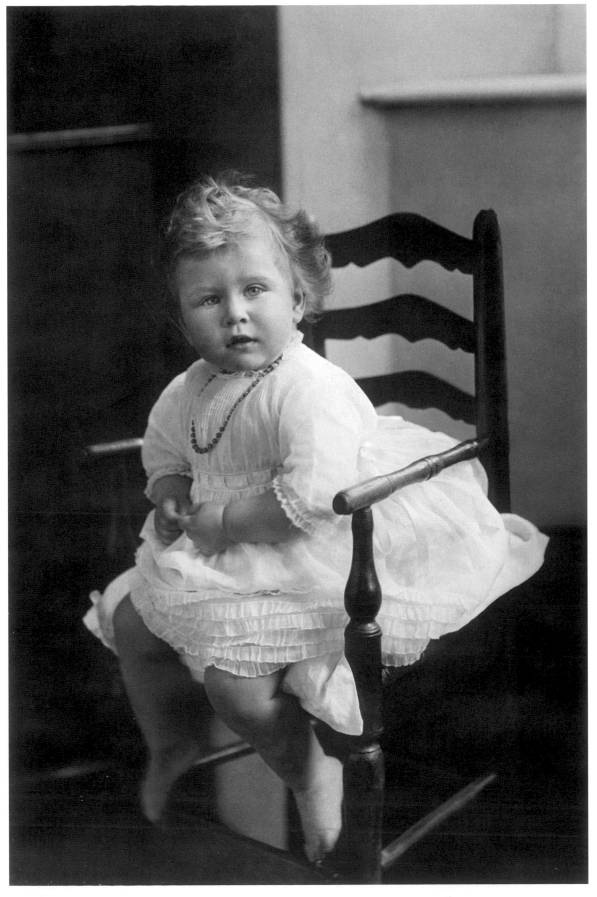

Queen Elizabeth II circa 1927, aged 18 months

The Duchess of York in a letter to her father-in-law King George V after the birth of her younger daughter Anne in August 1930.

'I am very anxious to call her Anne as I think Anne of York sounds so pretty'

Margaret

When '*Lilibet*' — a name that would always be used within the family — was almost three-and-a-half, the Duchess of York became pregnant again. As the pregnancy progressed she developed acrophobic tendencies. '*My instinct is to hide in a corner when in this condition,*' she told her mother-in-law Queen Mary some months before Margaret was born in August 1930. '*I suppose it is a feeling handed down from many generations back. I should really like to live quietly in the country for the last few months and then reappear afterwards as if nothing had happened.*' Elizabeth and Bertie wished their second child to be born in Scotland, at the iconic Glamis Castle — Elizabeth's ancestral home. In the middle of July, the family travelled to the castle in readiness for the birth, due to take place on August 8. By the end of July, the weather turned rainy and it was clear the mother-to-be was beginning to regret that she had not stayed in London. She wrote that the next time she had a baby she would try and give birth in London, in the winter. '*It is much more agreeable for both of us, I think, as when one is in the country one misses all the lovely flowers and cadeaux for the baby and little excitements like that,*' she wrote. On the evening of August 21, almost two weeks after her due date, the Duchess gave birth to another Princess after a relatively easy six hour labour while a storm raged outside. '*A very nice baby and everything went smoothly without any trouble,*' wrote Frank Reynolds, the Duchess' obstetrician and gynaecologist, to his wife. It had been reported, however, that the Duchess had been administered with the '*Twilight Sleep*' form of anaesthetic. This mix of morphine and scopolamine was widely used in childbirth from 1905 onwards. It didn't kill the pain of labour but the mother-to-be had no memory of it. These allegations were strenuously denied. The York's private secretary wrote to the press to protest that such stories were '*absolutely without any foundation and have caused Their Royal Highnesses the greatest possible annoyance.*'

The King and Queen were immediately informed of their new grand daughter's arrival with the Queen expressing slight disappointment that this baby wasn't a boy. However, the King did not seem to mind, commenting that little girls were more fun. Young Princess Elizabeth was apparently '*enchanted*' with her new baby sister, one of her maternal uncles noting that, '*first of all she thought it was a wonderful doll and then discovered it was alive. She then took each of the doctors present by the hand and said, "I want to introduce you to my baby sister".*' Father, Bertie, meanwhile although admitting he had wanted a son, wrote to his wife, '*I don't mind at all that it's a girl and Elizabeth now has a playmate in the nursery. We still have plenty of time, we are still young, although I think London in the Spring for the next one.*' In London, the usual gun salute was fired and the bells of Westminster Abbey and St Pauls pealed. But in Glamis, the birth of '*the lassie's bairn*' was celebrated with the lighting of a massive bonfire of larch, spruce

Right:
The Duchess of York is shown with her infant daughter, Princess Margaret Rose

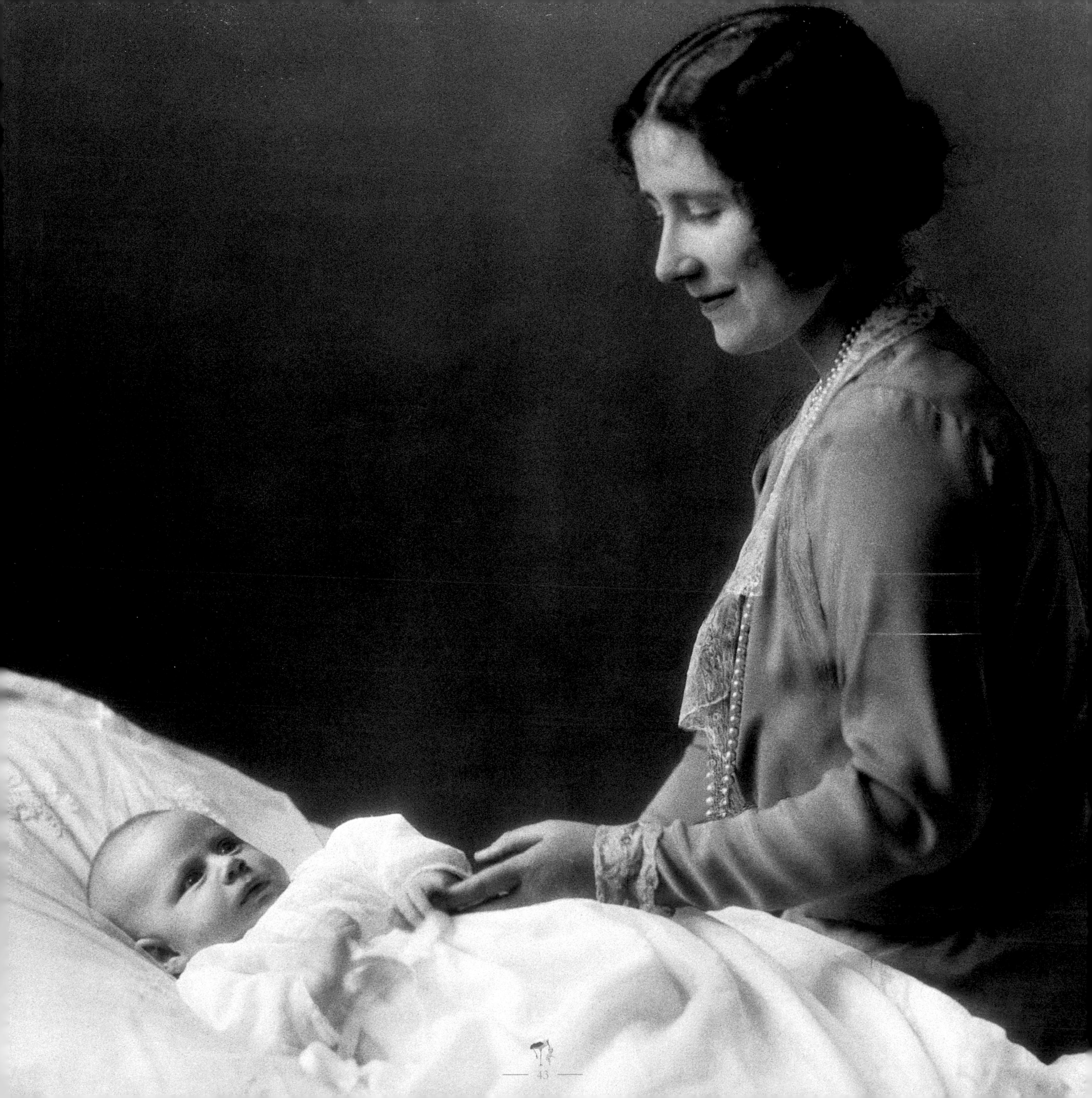

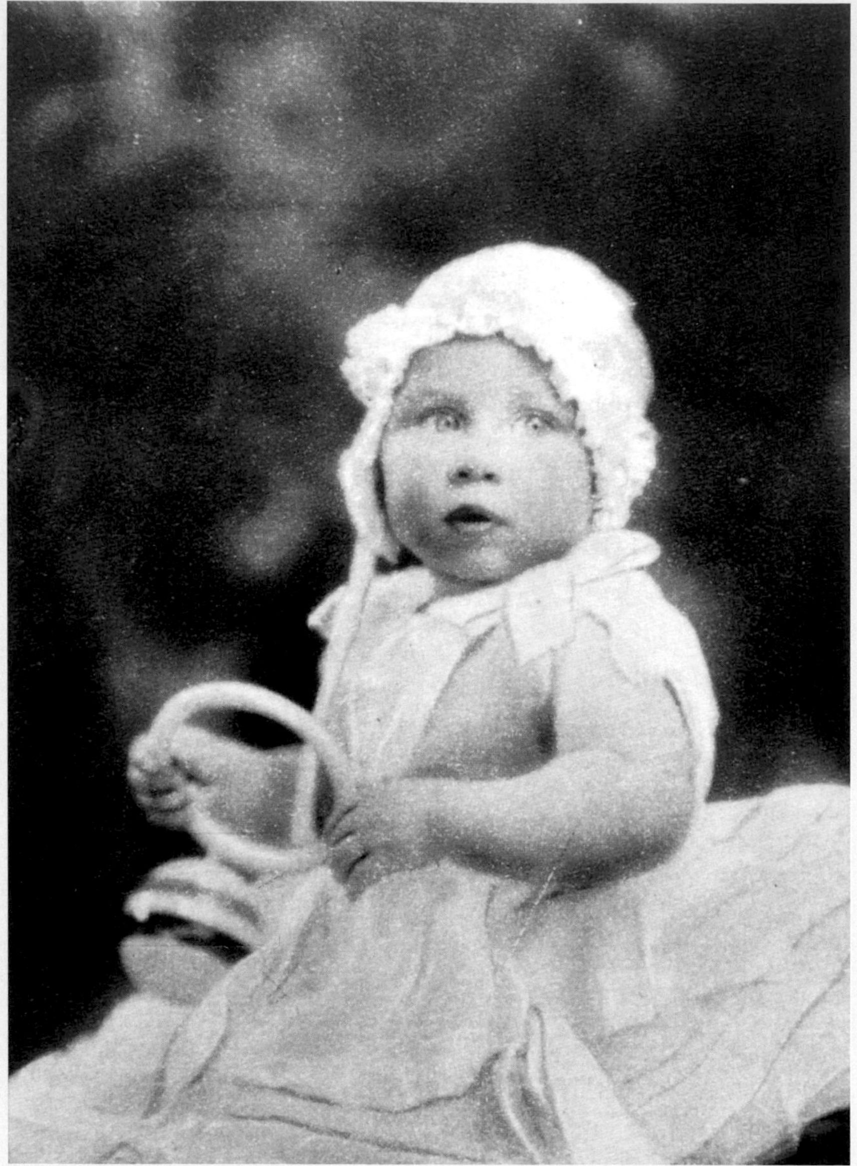

and oak branches. Lord Strathmore, the Duchess' father, provided barrels of beer for the crowds of well-wishers gathering at the castle gates.

The baby's birth was registered at the village shop in Glamis but the question of what to call her threw up some problems. '*I am very anxious to call her Anne as I think Anne of York sounds so pretty,*' wrote the Duchess to her father-in-law, George V. '*Lots of people have suggested Margaret but it has no family links on either side and besides, she will always be getting mixed up with Margaret the nursery maid*'. The Duchess may have thought Anne of York sounded '*so pretty*' but the King did not. He thought it a most '*unsuitable name*' and he had the final say. So, the baby was named Margaret — but with the fragrant '*Rose*' added as a second name. Her big sister, however, announced that she would be calling the baby '*Bud*' as she was not a fully-bloomed Rose yet. Next came the question of where Princess Margaret Rose would be christened. The Duchess' friend Cosmo Lang, who was the Archbishop of Canterbury, was coming to Balmoral and she wanted him to christen her newborn in the family chapel at Glamis, But it was felt that the Church of Scotland would not look kindly upon an Anglican Archbishop officiating at the christening of a Royal Princess who had, after all, been born in Scotland. The Duchess wasn't happy and felt too much fuss was being made. She wrote to Queen Mary, '*After all, the little angel is not of supreme importance at the moment. I always hope and pray that David will marry someone suitable. . .he ought to have some nice children*'. Lang came to Glamis to bless the baby but it was decided that the christening would take at the end of October in the private chapel at Buckingham Palace. The delay was due to the Duchess still being weak after the birth. '*It really does take a whole year to have a baby,*' she wrote to her mother-in-law at the end of September. '*I cannot manage much standing yet.*' Margaret Rose's god parents included her great aunt, Princess Victoria — the King's sister.

The new Princess joined her elder sister in the '*bright and airy*' nursery at 145 Piccadilly. She became Alah's main charge assisted by Bobo's sister, Ruby MacDonald, with Bobo caring for Lilibet. Alah loved having an infant to tend to once more and kept Margaret in baby-mode longer

Right:
The Duchess of York with the two Princesses Margaret Rose and Elizabeth. One of a selection of images from a family album taken in 1929-1930

Above:
The young Princess Margaret aged five months

than was necessary. It wasn't until the little Princess climbed out of her pram that the nanny was forced to accept that Margaret needed a modicum of independence. Precocious from a very early age, this is a baby that at nine-months-old was humming the waltz from '*The Merry Widow*' while being carried by her maternal grandmother. '*I was so astounded I almost dropped her,*' Lady Strathmore was to recall. Her parental grandmother was also entranced by her youngest grandchild. When the little Princesses were left with their grandparents for a short while at Sandringham in early 1933, Queen Mary wrote to their mother that Margaret, '*is a great pickle and does all kinds of things to annoy Papa (George V), though she seems to be very fond of him, she thinks it is funny and looks up at him with wicked eyes after she has done it — she is very attractive*'.

Having experienced a thoroughly miserable childhood, the Duke of York was determined that '*come what might, Princess Elizabeth and Princess Margaret should look upon their early years as a golden age*'. This was certainly the case until he unexpectedly came to the throne in late 1936. Margaret always felt she was her father's favourite. As a small child, she would wind her arms around his neck, nestle against him, cuddle and kiss him. Something the Duke had never felt able to do with either of his own parents. The children would see their '*mummy and papa*' as often as possible. Each morning, there would be fun and games in their parents' bedroom and in the evening, it would, whenever possible, be the Duke and Duchess overseeing bath and bed time. '*Hilarious sounds of splashing could be heard coming from the bathroom,*' said a Royal source. '*Later pillow fights would set the nanny begging the Duke and Duchess not to get the children too excited.*'

Right:
The one-year-old Prince Philip of Greece shows an interest in things floral

In contrast to the births and babyhoods of his future wife and sister-in-law, the arrival and early life of Prince Philip of Greece can only be described as chaotic. Named Philippos, this fifth child and only son of Prince and Princess Andrea of Greece, was born on June 10 1921 on the kitchen table in '*Mon Repos*', a rundown rented summer villa situated on the Greek island of Corfu. The house had no electricity, hot water or indoor plumbing and the family were so short of cash they had trouble finding the rent. It was several months before Andrea, a major-general in the Greek army, saw his son. Having at last been given the command of a division, he had left Athens for Smyrna the day before Philip's birth, accompanying his brother, King Constantine, who had placed himself at the head of his troops.

Nanny Roose Nicholas, known as '*Roosie*' took care of the baby Prince. She had raised his mother before him and was undoubtedly the greatest influence of his early life. His parents' marriage was unhappy and the family had no settled home so it was Nanny Roose who provided continuity and security. Before his birth in June 1921, she had had ordered supplies of British soap, British baby food and British woolies to be delivered to Corfu. Within 18 months of Philip's birth, however, the family were exiled and forced to leave the island with the baby travelling in a carry cot made from an old orange box. As they criss-crossed Europe in attempt to find a home, '*Roosie*' taught Philip English nursery rhymes and, although money was tight, dressed him in clothes sent from England. She insisted he speak English and observe English customs. She had her work cut out as he was a rascal. One of his favourite tricks was escaping from '*Roosie*' at bath time. He would run naked through the halls of whatever castle he happened to be living in at the time until someone finally caught him and brought him back to the bathtub. He was, said his sister, Princess Sophie, '*very active*'.

Princess Elizabeth the day after she became a mother for the first time

'I still find it difficult to believe that I have a baby of my own'

Charles, Anne, Andrew & Edward

Charles

Within a few months of her November 1947 marriage to Philip Duke of Edinburgh, Princess Elizabeth was pregnant. Not that any official announcement was made. She simply disappeared from view after making a state visit to Paris in May 1947 while three months pregnant and suffering from morning sickness. Six days short of her first wedding anniversary, on November 14 1948, the princess gave birth to her first child - a 7lb 6oz boy at 9.14pm. The Belgian Suite in Buckingham Palace was transformed into a temporary delivery room for the event with Elizabeth, attended by doctor Sir William Gilliatt and nursing sister Helen Rowe. Elizabeth had a tough time. After a 30 hour labour, the baby, thought to be breech, was born by Caesarian section. While his wife gave birth, the Duke of Edinburgh was smashing his way around a Squash court with an equerry. On hearing the news that he was a father, Philip grabbed the bouquet - roses, carnations and lilies — plus the bottle of champagne his equerry had ready for him, and raced up to the Belgian suite to see his wife and new born son. The second visitor was George VI who was so delighted his darling daughter Lilibet had given birth to a son and heir, he was heard cheering loudly as he entered the room.

Within an hour of the birth, the following announcement was attached to the Buckingham Palace railings. *'Her Royal Highness the Princess Elizabeth, Duchess of Edinburgh, was safely delivered of a Prince at 9.14 o'clock this evening. Her Royal Highness and the infant Prince are both doing well.'* Upwards of three thousand people waiting outside the gates broke into a rendition of '*For He's a Jolly Good Fellow.*' A 40-gun salute was fired in Hyde Park, the bells of St Paul's and Westminster Abbey rang out for three hours, bonfires were lit across the country and the fountains in Trafalgar Square ran blue. By the next day, more than 4000 telegrams from well-wishers had been received at the Palace — in addition to many hand-knitted baby clothes and toys. The new mother was enchanted with her baby, noting that his hands were '*fine with long fingers — quite unlike mine and certainly unlike his fathers — it will be interesting to see what they become. I still find it difficult to believe that I have a baby of my own.*' The new father's reaction to his new born son was rather less prosaic. When asked who his son looked like, Philip replied, '*A plum pudding!*' Elizabeth breast fed her baby for the first few weeks of his life and during this time he slept in a wicker basket situated in his mother's dressing room which adjoined her bedroom.

The new Prince who was third in line to the throne was named Charles Philip Arthur George. This was regarded as a brave choice at the time as Charles was still viewed as an unlucky Royal name, a Stuart name. Charles I had been beheaded, Charles II had a chequered past and womanizing reputation yet had been unable to provide the country with an heir, and his great nephew, Charles Edward Stuart,

Right:
Princess Elizabeth with her baby son Prince Charles

Left:
Prince Charles at five-weeks-old

'*Bonnie Prince Charlie,*' had died a penniless alcoholic in exile. It was, however, Elizabeth's favourite name. Wearing the satin and lace gown passed down from the 1840s, baby Charles was christened on December 15 1948 in the White and Gold Music Room at Buckingham Palace. His god parents included his grandfather George VI, great grandmother Queen Mary, the King of Norway and Prince George of Greece. There were three christening cakes which were displayed in the White Drawing Room at Buckingham Palace, where a family reception was held after the ceremony. The principal cake was - as tradition dictated - the top tier of his parents' wedding cake, although it had been redecorated. It featured intricate lace work done in icing and was topped with a silver cradle in which a '*baby doll dressed by the Royal School of Art Needlework in a christening robe*' slept. Students from the National Bakery School concocted the second confection - a sturdy, square-shaped cake topped with a coronet. The third cake was comprised of two tiers and was decorated with small silver charms and other silver ornaments made by war-disabled, ex-service silversmiths. Lastly, a smaller cake, made for a '*private celebration*' was baked by a Mrs. Barnes, the cook at Prince Charles' parents' rented country house, Windlesham Moor in Berkshire. Mrs. Barnes *'was obliged to limit the amount of sugar in the cake'* due to war-time rations that were still in effect. To mark the occasion, Elizabeth asked that food parcels be sent to every British mother who had also given birth on November 14. Cakes and food parcels apart, Queen Mary was thrilled with her great-grandson and godson. She wrote in her diary on the day of the christening: '*I gave the baby a silver gilt cup & cover which George III had given to a godson in 1780*', and added proudly '*I gave a present from my great grandfather, to my great grandson 168 years later.*'

By the time of his christening, baby Charles was adapting to his nursery routine. The large sunny room that had once been the school room for his mother and his aunt Margaret had been turned into a nursery. Charles' cot was a miniature four-poster brought down from the attic and about 400-years-old. His pram had been used by his mother and aunt, and even his first toy — an ivory-handled rattle — had been shaken by earlier Royal babies. The nursery was the domain of Nanny Helen Lightbody. A Royal Nanny in the '*Alah/Bobo*' mold, this Scottish-born daughter of an Edinburgh textile worker was known as '*no nonsense Lightbody,*' yet she was thought to have been very kind and fair. Charles adored her and his first word is thought to have been '*Nana*', his name for her. It was Nana who got Charles up in the morning and dressed him — just as '*Alah*' had done with his mother.

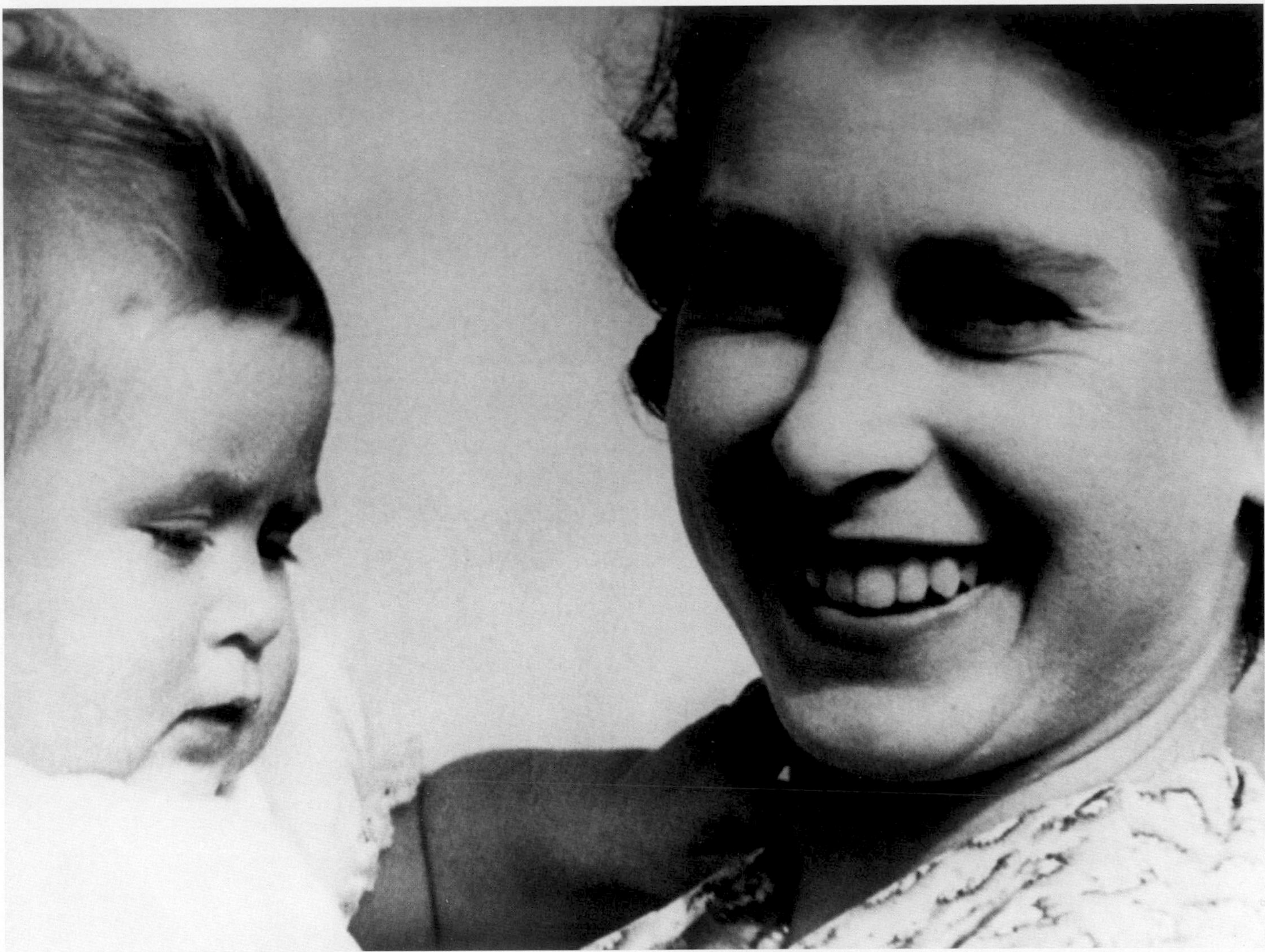

Nana also slept in the same room as little Charles and comforted him when he awoke in the night. She left Royal service under something of a cloud in 1956 — it's said the Queen fired her because she overruled the Queen had ordered for Prince Charles' dinner. Mabel Anderson, '*No-nonsense Lightbody's*' assistant and a policeman's daughter from Scotland, joined the Royal Household in 1949 as assistant nanny — the then Princess Elizabeth liking Mabel's quiet, unassuming manner. Prince Charles was to describe her as '*a haven of security, the greatest haven — warm, loving sympathetic and caring*'. Curiously, Mabel — or Mipsy as Charles called her - in her younger years is said to have resembled Camilla, and it has been suggested that this was, in part, the reason Charles fell in love with his second wife! Now in her 90s, Mabel retains a grace-and-favour apartment near Windsor Castle. Each Christmas, Charles sends a chauffeur-driven car to take Mabel to Sandringham, where she is treated like a cherished member of the family rather than an employee.

As a mother Elizabeth was loving but distant. By the time Charles was three-months-old, she had begun her routine of seeing her son twice a day — for an hour after breakfast and for about 30 minutes in the evening. When engagements allowed, she would watch him being bathed — although it's not thought she actually got her hands wet. It

Left:
Prince Charles is pushed around Green Park in his pram by his nanny on his second birthday

was Mipsy who took Charles out in his pram, put him to bed, read him stories, taught him to say his prayers and brush his teeth. In 1949, Charles moved into Clarence House with his parents. His nursery had white and pale blue walls, white chintz curtains and covers with black-line drawings of nursery rhyme figures on them. There was a glass-fronted cabinet for his toy horses, soldiers and teddy bears — many of which had belonged to his mother.

In November 1949, Charles was left in London while his mother travelled to Malta to join her husband who was there on naval duty. She stayed away for six weeks, missing Charles' first birthday and first Christmas which he spent with his grandparents, his first tooth, first word — '*Nana*' rather than '*Mama*' - and his first step. '*He is too sweet for words stomping around the room,*' George VI wrote to his daughter. Elizabeth returned to the UK at the end of December and discovered she was pregnant again. In March 1950, she took off to Malta for a second time — once again leaving Charles with his grandparents and nanny. For Elizabeth, it wasn't a big deal rather just what '*one*' did. She had been brought up in a similar way - as a nine-month-old baby she had been left by her parents for six months while they toured the globe. Two months later, she was back to await the birth of her second child who was due that August. '*Both Philip and I are thrilled about the new baby,*' she wrote to a friend. *We only hope Charles will take kindly to it.*'

Prince Philip's verdict on his newborn daughter

'It's the sweetest girl'

Anne

Princess Anne Elizabeth Louise was born at Clarence House on August 15 1950 at 11.50am, weighing 6lbs. At 3.30 that afternoon, a Royal Salute was fired in Hyde Park by the King's Troop of the Royal Horse Artillery. Prince Philip, who that day had learned that he had achieved his life-long ambition and been given command of his own ship, bought champagne for staff to wet the baby's head. The baby Princess was visited twice by her grandmother on the day of her birth, although her grandfather George VI was away shooting in Balmoral. As for her big brother, it seems he did take kindly to the new arrival. Whenever visitors arrived, he would take them by the hand and want to show them the new baby. The newborn slept in her father's dressing room for a few weeks while her mother breast fed her. Before Philip joined his ship, the registrar came to Clarence House to register the baby's birth and complete her birth certificate. Afterwards, Philip was presented with Anne's identity card, a ration book, and bottles of cod liver oil and orange juice.

Princess Anne was christened in the Music Room of Buckingham Palace by Dr Cyril Garbett, Archbishop of York on October 21 1950. As well as the then Princess Elizabeth, the Duke of Edinburgh, King George VI, Queen Elizabeth, and Queen Mary, also present were Princess Anne's godparents - Earl Mountbatten (uncle of the Duke of Edinburgh), Princess Margarita, Princess of Hohenlohe-Langenburg (sister of the Duke of Edinburgh), Andrew Elphinstone (cousin of Princess Elizabeth), and Princess Alice,

Left:
Princess Elizabeth with her husband, Prince Philip, and their children Prince Charles and the baby Princess Anne

Countess of Athlone (great-aunt of Princess Elizabeth). Philip joined his ship a few days later. A few weeks later — baby Anne having joined Charles in the nursery under the watchful eye of '*Nana*' and '*Mipsy*' — their mother took off for Malta again to join her husband. She stayed there for three months, again missing Christmas with her children who had gone to Sandringham with their grandparents.

by the time Anne was a-year-old, she was developing into quite a character. With her curly blonde hair, she may have looked like butter wouldn't melt but she was, unlike her quieter, more introspective brother, quite a handful. In the early years, Charles was protective of his little sister, though he would scold her when she misbehaved. '*You are such a trouble to me,*' he would say. Anne was adventurous. She never hid behind her mother's skirts or hung on to her nanny's hand. She'd crawl off on her own to explore, seemingly having no fear. It is a trait that has served her well throughout her life. As a small child, the clothes she wore became instantly popular — much as Prince George and Princess Charlotte's do today. As a two-year-old, the knitted jacket she wore became the jacket to be worn by the young!

'Andrew has gorgeous fat little legs'

Prince Andrew's nursery assistant shortly after his birth in 1960

Andrew

The Queen found out she was pregnant for a third time just as she was to embark on a nine-week tour of Canada in mid 1959. It wasn't a problem, though. Ever practical, she took a dressmaker with her, skilled in discreetly letting out the '*Royal*' wardrobe. She and Philip had long wanted a third child and had been trying for a baby for two or three years. They were delighted when Prince Andrew Albert Christian Edward arrived 10 years after his sister, Anne. Weighing 7lb 3oz, he was born in the same mocked-up delivery room in Buckingham Palace as his brother, arriving on the afternoon of February 19 1960 - his father hid away in his study as his mother gave birth. He was the first child to be born to a reigning monarch in 103 years. In time honoured tradition, there was a 21 gun salute in Hyde Park plus a fly past of 36 Hunter jets over Buckingham Palace. Soon after Andrew's birth, Elizabeth wrote to her second cousin, Lady Mary Cambridge, '*The baby is adorable and is very good, and putting on weight well. Both the elder children are completely riveted by him and all in all, he's going to be terribly spoiled by all of us, I'm sure.*' From the moment of Andrew's birth, his mother made time for him, cutting short engagements, postponing tours and spending long periods in the Buckingham Palace nursery.

Initially there were concerns that '*something was wrong*' with the little Prince as there was so little news of him and no photos. But the Queen and the Duke had decided that their third child should be brought up as quietly and privately as possible. He was christened in the Music Room at

Above:

Elizabeth II with her son Prince Andrew in a pram and Princess Anne September 1960

Right:

Queen Elizabeth II and Prince Philip with their baby son, Prince Edward, on the balcony at Buckingham Palace, during the Trooping of the Colour, London, 13th June 1964

Right:
Queen Elizabeth, the Queen Mother (1900-2002) sits with her grandchildren Prince Charles, Princess Anne and baby Prince Andrew

Left:
New born Prince Andrew in Queen Elizabeth II's arms

Buckingham Palace on April 8 1960 with Princess Alexandra among his god parents. There were no official christening photos, although thanks to the correspondence of new nursery assistant, Lincolnshire-born June Waller, we have some insight into what happened on the day. The little prince pee'ed on her! '*He christened me before we went,*' she wrote in her journal. '*I had him on his pot, not thinking, of course. He misaimed and I went to the royal christening with a damp skirt!! I'm not used to little boys yet!*'

As she had done with Charles and Anne, the Queen breast fed her new-born for the first few weeks before he was introduced to the nursery on the second floor of Buckingham Palace. Mabel was now in charge, aided by June, with her letters written to a friend, providing a fascinating glimpse of life in the Buckingham Palace Nursery. '*Andrew has gorgeous fat little legs. Really he's a poppet. He's doing well and now weighs 9lb 9oz. He's on half-cream Cow & Gate milk.*' She wrote. '*The other evening, I had the Queen, Duke, Princess Royal (Elizabeth II's aunt), Duchess of Kent (Elizabeth II's aunt), Lady Brabourne [Patricia, Countess Mountbatten of Burma] and Lady Abergavenny [lady-in-waiting to the Queen] all sitting round the nursery fire watching me give Andrew his supper!! It was terrible. I should think I can face anything after that! I had to will myself not to let my hand shake! I also had A. A. Jones [who married Princess Margaret and became Lord Snowdon] and the Queen up one night to photograph Andrew in the bath. It was really terribly funny, he had just started and the camera stuck. Poor Andrew, he was in the bath about 20 minutes while adjustments were carried out. Even the Queen said, "Well, he'll shrivel up if he stays in here much longer." He took some pictures of him wrapped up in a towel with the Queen holding him (she was sitting on the 'loo' for want of a better place), then lying on his tummy on my lap being dried, then looking angelic in his nightie.*' By the time he was six months old, Sister Helen Rowe remarked that

Andrew was '*a baby full of smiles, simply wonderful in every respect.*'

In September 1960, when Andrew was seven-months-old, June wrote from Balmoral, '*This morning he weighed 21lb 14oz. We have now run out of weights - next week we shall have to borrow from the kitchen! He cut another tooth today making seven and there is another one almost through. So by the 19th he should have eight teeth - which, according to all good books, is correct.*'

Held in his mother's arms, Andrew, dressed in an embroidered romper suit, made his first balcony appearance aged 16 months for the Queen's official birthday parade in June 1961. He grew into a confident, loving but often naughty little boy. Mabel '*Mipsy*' Anderson remarked that no nursery would ever be able to cope with two Prince Andrews. When Andrew was three-years-old, he was told he was getting a playmate who would turn out to be a new baby brother. . .

The Queen after the birth of Prince Edward

'Goodness, what fun it is to have a baby in the house again'

Edward

The Queen went into labour a week before her fourth and final child was due. It hadn't been an easy pregnancy with Elizabeth, now 37, being instructed to rest for much of it. At 8.20pm on March 10 1964, the baby Prince was born — like his two brothers - in the Belgian Suite at Buckingham Palace, weighing just 5lb 7oz. In a break with tradition, the Duke of Edinburgh was actually holding his wife's hand as their youngest was born. The Queen had asked him to be there. She had been keenly reading women's magazines that stressed the importance of involving fathers in childbirth and had become fascinated by the idea. Thus, Philip became the first Royal father in modern history to witness the arrival of one of his children. '*Goodness what fun it is to have a baby in the house again,*' the Queen told a friend. '*He is a great joy to us all, especially Andrew who is completely fascinated by him. In fact, he considers him his own property, even telling Charles and Anne to "come and see my baby"!*'

Both the Queen and Duke had expected the baby to be a girl and had, discussed only girls' names. They decided on Edward as a first name but decided his other Christian names should be a tribute to his godfathers — Antony after his uncle Antony Armstrong Jones, Richard after Prince Richard of Gloucester, and Louis after Prince Louis of Hesse. His godmothers were Prince Philip's sister Sophie and the Duchess of Kent. Baby Edward was christened in the private chapel at Windsor Castle on May 2 1964.

The Queen was noticeably more relaxed with her younger children than she had been with her first two. She blossomed as a mother

Right:
The Queen and Prince Philip with their four children in 1965

Above:
The two youngest children of Queen Elizabeth, Prince Andrew, left, and baby, Prince Edward

Right:
Queen Elizabeth II and Prince Philip, Duke of Edinburgh and their children at Windsor on the Queen's 39th birthday, April 1965

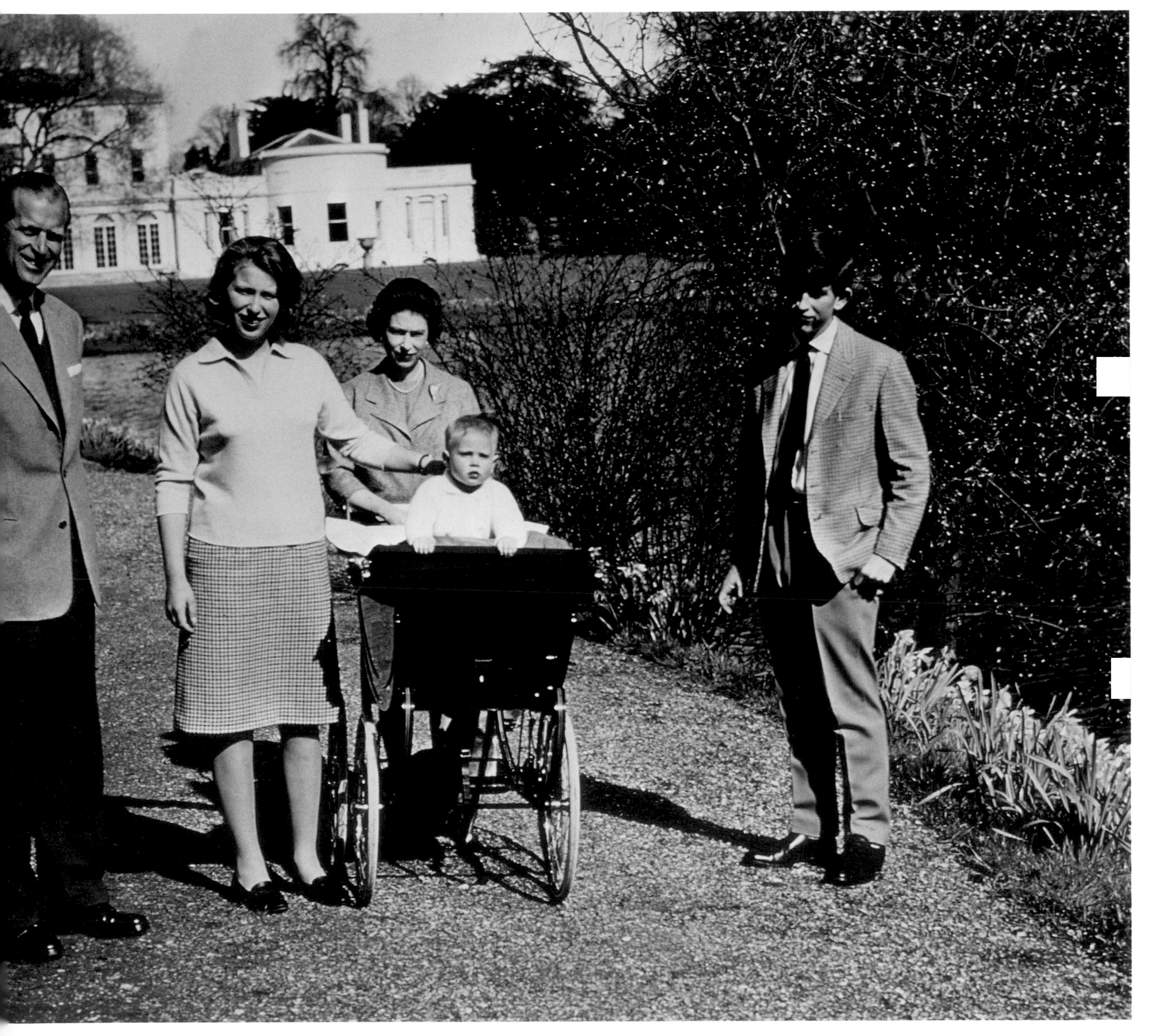

and liked to spend as much time as she could with her small sons. She would ask the nanny to leave Edward playing on the floor of the study as she went over state papers at her desk. Life in the Royal nursery, however, went on pretty much as it had before with Mipsy looking after the new charge, assisted by June Waller. When Edward was eight months old June described him as '*an absolute poppet*', '*a funny, cheeky little thing — not a bit like Andrew.*' She went on to reveal, '*He has four teeth, weighed 20lb 8oz last week and shoots across the floor like a rocket on his elbows and knees and tummy. London being what it is, the colour of his clothes is nobody's business. In fact, he looks permanently like a scruffy, cheeky little London sparrow, except when he is clean in bed. Andrew adores him - he has right from the first moment. He hauls him out of mischief (i.e. the TV flex) by his feet and drags him to the other side of the room. The baby adores it and scuffles back for more rough treatment.*' He was, it seems, a very appealing little chap. '*Quite the quietest,*' said his mother. '*And isn't it unfair a boy should have such long eyelashes.*' It is probable that this little Prince had the happiest upbringing of all of the Queen's children.

One Princess who most definitely did not have a happy childhood was the girl born Lady Diana Spencer on July 1 1961. She was born the year after the brother she never knew had died within hours of his birth. Although her father, the heir to the Spencer earldom, pronounced her a '*perfect physical specimen*', he and his wife Frances were noticeably disappointed that this fourth child (they already had two daughters, Sarah and Jane) was female. '*I was supposed to be a boy,*' Diana was later to say. She knew that if her elder brother had lived, she would never have been born. By the time she was five-years-old, her parents' marriage was over — her mother having left her father for wallpaper heir, Peter Shand-Kydd. A vicious tug of love ensued with her mother and father going to court to fight for custody of their four children (the longed-for son and heir, Charles, having finally arrived in 1964). Frances' mother, Ruth Lady Fermoy, testified against her own daughter with the result that the children were awarded to their father. According to the children's nanny, Nanny Clarke, Diana was '*seriously affected*' by the breakdown of her parents' marriage and the subsequent fall-out. It was, she was later to say, '*A very painful experience and a very unhappy childhood*'.

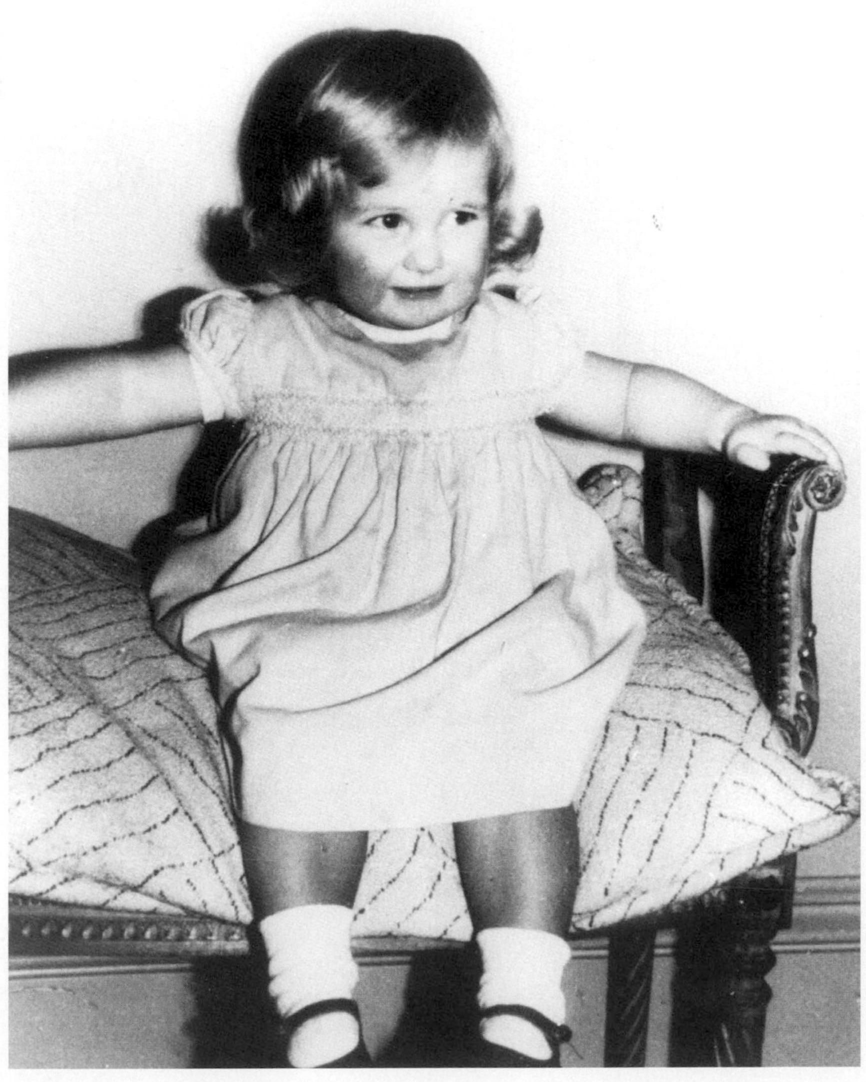

Above:
Lady Diana Frances Spencer, later Princess of Wales, aged two, at Park House, Sandringham, Norfolk

Opp Page:
Lady Diana Frances Spencer, later Princess of Wales, on her first birthday at Park House, Sandringham

'If men had babies, they would only have one each'

William and Harry

Within a year of her marriage to the Prince of Wales in July 1981, Princess Diana, aged just 20, had done her dynastic duty and given birth to a son and heir. She had fallen pregnant while on extended honeymoon at Balmoral. '*Thank heavens for William,*' she later said. Naturally both she and the Prince were delighted but it was a far from an easy pregnancy. Diana suffered from extreme morning sickness plus she was still prone to bouts of bulimia which blighted her early years as a Royal. Over the Christmas and New Year break of 1982/3 at Sandringham House, Diana, then three months pregnant, fell down the stairs. Whether done on purpose as a '*cry for help*' or a genuine accident, fortunately Diana was not seriously hurt and despite some abdominal bruising, a full check-up by George Pinker, her gynaecologist, revealed the baby was fine. In February 1982, when she was five months pregnant, her husband whisked her away to the Bahamas for a '*babymoon*'. '*What Diana needs is a holiday in the sunshine to prepare for the birth,*' commented Prince Charles. However, the trip turned sour after a bikini-clad Diana and Charles, in swimming shorts, were snapped by paparazzi, embracing on the beach and jumping the waves. The photos were splashed across the British tabloids. The Queen was furious, provoking her to comment through her press secretary that, '*this is one of the blackest days in British journalism*'. She later received an apology. The rest of Diana's pregnancy passed without incident. The morning sickness stopped, she developed a passion for bacon and tomato sandwiches, and appeared more in public — usually in one of the smock dresses she so loved to wear. Polka dot smocks, designer smocks, coat smocks, frilly smocks, plain smocks. . . the pregnancy smock market really swelled as a result.

Unable to cope with increasing press intrusion as her due date approached, Diana decided to have her baby induced a week early. *'It's well cooked,'* she told a friend and on June 20, she and Charles arrived at the private Lindo wing of St Mary's Hospital in Paddington, west London. '*I was as sick as a parrot the whole way through labour,*' Diana revealed. When her temperature rose dramatically, Mr Pinker and his team considered performing an emergency Caesarean section. However, Diana was given an epidural injection to numb the pangs of child birth. After a 16-hour labour, at 9.03pm on June 21, with Prince Charles at her side, Diana gave birth to a 7lb 1½oz baby boy — the first heir to the British throne ever to be born in a hospital. He had a wisp of blonde hair and blue eyes, and according to his besotted father was '*beautiful*' and '*in marvellous form*'. In a letter, he wrote to his godmother, Patricia Brabourne, Prince Charles expressed his joy at having been present at the birth of his son, saying: '*I am so thankful I was beside Diana's bedside the whole time because by the end of the day I really felt as though I'd shared deeply in the process of birth. The birth of our son has made me incredibly proud and somewhat amazed.*' Diana was just as in love with her baby boy. '*The first time I experienced true happiness was when I held William in my arms,*' she was to reveal.

In celebration of baby Wales' birth, the Hussars of the Royal Horse Artillery fired the traditional 41-gun salute, and when his paternal grandmother visited her new grandson and heir the next day, she commented, '*Thank goodness he hasn't got ears like his father.*' Twenty-four hours after the birth, Diana — still dressed in one of her maternity smocks, Charles and their baby boy left hospital. '*Baby Wales*' would not have a name for several more days as his parents could not agree. '*We're having a little argument about what to call him,*' Charles admitted to reporters. Charles wished to call his first-born son Arthur but Diana preferred William. They eventually decided on William Arthur Philip Louis, honouring William the Conqueror, King Arthur, the Duke of Edinburgh and Lord Louis Mountbatten. He was known as '*Wills*' by his doting parents plus to Diana, he was '*Wombat*'. In recognition of his wife's deliverance, Charles gifted Diana with several *'push presents'* or '*baby baubles*' — a necklace of diamonds and cultured pearls with a sparkling heart at its centre, a solid gold '*W*' for her charm bracelet and a brand new, custom-built Mini in apple green with a convertible foldaway roof and enough room for a collapsible cot.

Back home at Kensington Palace, the nursery, decorated with red, white and blue rabbits, was ready and in pristine condition. Diana breast fed William for two months while Charles was so smitten by his son, he cancelled some of his engagements to stay at home — much to the derision of his father, the Duke of Edinburgh. He changed William's nappy, played with him and bathed him. In fact, Charles and William regularly shared a bath. One evening when Diana and Charles were supposed to be going to an engagement, she found her husband in the bath with their baby son. '*They were having a great time,*' she said. '*There was soap and water everywhere.*' It was not all sweetness and light, however. Not only had Charles and Diana argued about William's name, they also were rowing about nannies. Charles wanted his old nanny, Mabel Anderson, to help take care of the baby but Diana, who had been an assistant at a nursery school before her marriage, did not agree. She felt that Mabel was too old and too traditional. If Diana had to have a nanny take care of her son when she was unable to, she was adamant it should be someone she could relate to and who had similar ideas. Barbara Barnes, who had looked after the children of Princess

Above Left & Main Image:
New born Prince William leaves St Mary's Hospital with his parents, the Prince and Princess of Wales

Left:
Diana, Princess of Wales holds Prince William as Prince Charles looks on during their son's christening in the Music Room at Buckingham Palace on August 4 1982

Right:
Diana, Princess of Wales and Prince Charles with their baby son at Kensington Palace in December 1982

Margaret's close friends, Lord and Lady Glenconner, was hired and was the first royal nanny not to have been formally trained or to have had at least two nursery footmen and two nursemaids to help her. '*I am here to help, not to take over,*' she said shortly after her appointment. And Diana needed help. She was a tactile mother but her bulimia had returned, she was suffering from post-natal depression and she was forever fretting about her baby. '*Is he alright, Barbara?*' she would ask over and over again. Ironically, Diana would later become jealous of the bond William and Barbara shared. As a toddler, he would climb into '*Baba's*' bed before breakfast every morning.

William's christening took place at 11am on August 4 1982 in the Music Room at Buckingham Palace. Like all Royal babies since the time of Queen Victoria, he was dressed in the ornate christening gown of Spitalfields' silk satin and Honiton lace. The Archbishop of Canterbury officiated and William's six god parents - Princess Alexandra, the Queen's lady in waiting Lady Susan Hussey, ex-King Constantine of Greece, Lord Romsey grandson of Lord Louis Mountbatten, South African philosopher Sir Laurens Van der Post, and the Duchess of Westminster — were very much Charles' choice. Diana looked beautiful in a pink ensemble but the christening wasn't exactly a happy occasion for her. '*I was treated like nobody else's business,*' she was later to say. '*Nobody asked me if it was suitable for William — 11 o'clock couldn't have been worse. Endless pictures of the Queen, the Queen Mother, Charles and William. I was excluded that day. I wasn't very well and I just blubbed my eyes out. William started crying, too. Well, he just sensed that I wasn't exactly hunky dory.*'

At six months, William attended his first proper press conference when TV cameras were allowed into Kensington Palace to witness the baby prince gurgling and playing with his toes. When he was nine-months-old, his parents were due to tour Australia and New Zealand for six weeks. But whereas the Queen, and George VI and Queen Elizabeth, the Queen Mother, had left their off spring for months on end in order to go overseas, there was no way Diana was going to let that happen.

All Above:
Prince William & Diana pose for portraits in the sitting room of their home in Kensington Palace

Above Right & Main Image:

Diana Princess of Wales and Prince Charles with new born Prince Harry, leave St Mary's on September 16 1984

'*You know how you felt,*' Diana told Charles. '*You were miserable when your mother left you for months at a time and you were older than Wills. I will not do that to him. I know he's just a baby but he still needs our attention.*' The Queen was thought to be dubious when Prince Charles broached the subject with his mother but happily, Malcolm Fraser, the then Australian Prime Minister, wrote to Diana, suggesting that she and Charles bring their baby boy — and his nanny-along. '*It was wonderful,*' said Diana. '*We didn't see much of him but at least we were under the same sky, so to speak.*'

It has been rumoured that Diana suffered a miscarriage in September 1983 but whether or not she did, she fell pregnant again at the end of that year. Once again, she suffered from morning sickness although not so badly as before. However, the second half of the pregnancy was, in Diana's words, '*Blissful — Charles and I were getting along better than we ever had.*' This time she didn't gain excess weight like she had with William and her maternity wardrobe was rather more stylish but. . . she was harbouring a secret. She knew Charles desperately wanted a baby daughter but a scan had revealed she was carrying another boy. She chose not to tell her husband. After a nine-hour, drug-free labour, Diana and Charles' second son was born at 4.20pm on September 15 in the Lindo wing at St Mary's hospital. Charles had been an exemplary birth partner during the labour — staying by his wife's side throughout, moping her brow, rubbing her back and feeding her ice cubes. But, according to Diana, his reaction to the new born was disappointment rather than jubilation. '*Oh God, it's a boy,*' Diana revealed were his words, '*and he's even got red hair.*' Diana was later to tell friends, '*Something inside me closed off.*' Charles left the hospital shortly after the birth and, having picked a very glamorous, newly-coiffed Diana - plus baby - the next morning, he spent the rest of day on the polo field. '*Our marriage, the whole thing went down the drain,*' was Diana's verdict. On a happier note, the new born prince received an antique baby piano from singer Barry Manilow!

As she had done with William, Diana breast fed Harry for two months. This time, at least, there were no arguments about the baby's name — officially he would be called Henry Charles Albert David — but he would always be known as Harry. The new Prince was christened at St George's Chapel, Windsor on December 21 1984. Official photos released to coincide with the christening showed the new Royal quartet looking for all the world like the perfect nuclear family. In a first for a Royal christening, TV cameras recorded extraordinary footage of the Royal Family inside Windsor Castle - Diana, looking stunning in cobalt blue, as she cradled her baby son; cheeky two-and-a-half-year-

Above:
Prince Harry is carried by his nanny, Barbara Barnes, onto the Royal flight leaving Aberdeen airport in Scotland on March 25 1985

Right:
Surrounded by Royal relatives and godparents who are amused at the antics of young Prince William, Prince Harry is christened at Windsor Castle on December 21 1984

Above Left:

Prince William attempting to give baby brother, Prince Harry, a helping hand as he takes his first steps at their home in Kensington Palace

Above Right:

Prince William giggles with his hand-over-his-mouth as he and baby brother, Harry, pretend to plays the piano during a private photo session at home in Kensington Palace

Right:

Prince Charles with one-year-old Prince Harry at home in Kensington Palace

old Prince William charging up and down the gallery with his cousins Peter and Zara Phillips; the Queen Mother regal in royal purple. . . Diana insisted on choosing the female god parents for Harry but her selection reportedly caused a rift in the family. Charles had suggested that his one and only sister Princess Anne be one of the god mothers but Diana refused to consider it. She wanted women she could relate to — and she and the brusque, no-nonsense Anne were chalk and cheese. Diana chose her friend, chief bridesmaid and cousin-in-law Lady Sarah Armstrong Jones; Carolyn Bartholomew, former flatmate from her bachelor girl days; and a friend, Lady Celia Vestey. Charles chose his brother Andrew, artist Bryan Organ, and rich polo player Gerald Ward. Anne was so humiliated at being passed over as a god parent that she declined to attend the christening, saying the date clashed with a shooting party that she and husband, Captain Mark Phillips had planned. She refused to reschedule when asked by the Queen's press secretary. '*So what?*' she is reported to have said. '*Peter and Zara will be there — and that will be quite enough.*' This wasn't the only christening clash. Prince Charles felt the sharp end of his mother-in-law's tongue when he complained about the baby being a boy. '*He went to talk to my mother at Harry's christening and said, "I'm so disappointed — I thought it would be a girl*', Diana said. '*Mummy snapped his head off, saying, "You should be thankful that you had a child that was normal".*'

Barbara Barnes now had two Royal Princes under her care in the top floor nursery at Kensington Palace — but it wasn't to be for that much longer. There are conflicting rumours as to why '*Baba*' left the Wales' employ in late 1986 — Diana was still jealous of the nanny and wanted the boys to herself, Barbara got tired of Diana's constant interfering, or that the Queen had insisted that a stricter nanny be employed. After Barbara's departure, there was a succession of temporary nannies but then under-nanny Olga Powell took charge, giving the boys a steady routine. They were, she said, '*Just like any other children. Their upbringing was very normal and their parents wanted them to have as ordinary a childhood as they could.*' As babies and then young children,

Left:
Princess Diana cuddling her baby son, Prince Harry, aboard the Royal Yacht Britannia during her tour of Italy in May 1985

Right:
Prince Harry learning to crawl at home in Kensington Palace, October 1985

the Princes were developing quite different personalities. William was a fractious baby to begin with, turning into a solemn little soul who then morphed into a rumbustious toddler who delighted in throwing items such as his father's shoes down the toilet. Baby Harry, however, was calm, placid and, in his first few years, shyer and more subdued than his boisterous older brother.

As her marriage began to break down, Diana became ever more devoted to her boys. She was an imaginative, hands-on mother and her sons were the absolute lights of her life. Diana would refuse to go on tour for more than three weeks at a time if it meant being away from them and she'd call them at least once a day when she was. Hugs and cuddles were a constant. *'I hug my children to death and get into bed with them at night,'* she said. *'I want to bring them security and always feed them love and affection — it's so important.'* In 2017, Prince Harry spoke very touchingly of those embraces from his mother who had tragically passed away 20 years before when he was just 12-years-old. *'She would just engulf you and squeeze you as tight as possible. And being as short as I was then, there was no escape, you were there and you were there for as long as she wanted to hold you ...*

... Even talking about it now I can feel the hugs that she used to give us and I miss that. I miss that feeling.'

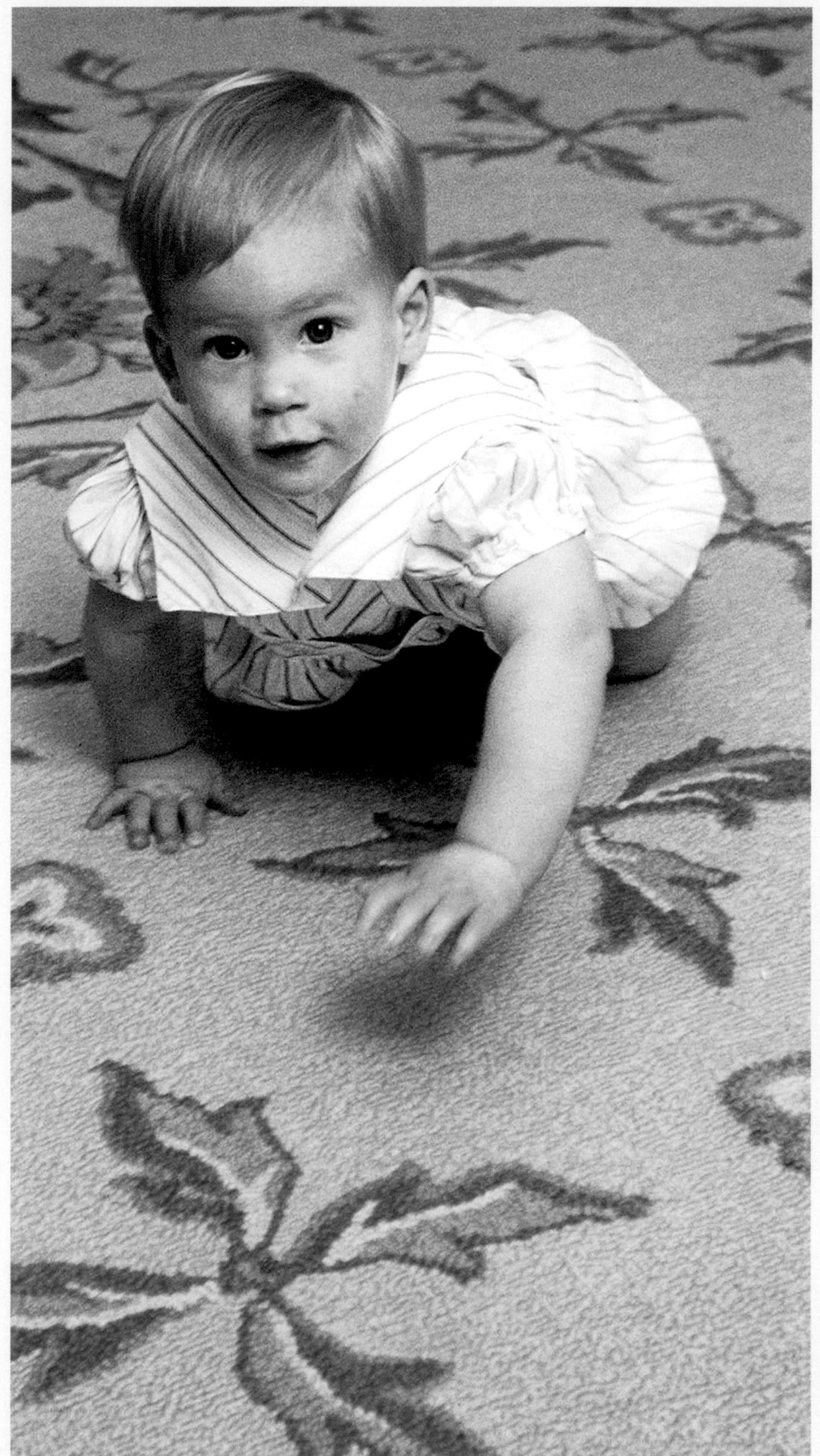

The Duke and Duchess of Cambridge's affectionate term for the unborn Prince George

'Our Little Grape'

Cambridge Babies

Prince George

On December 3 2012, Clarence House announced that the Duke and Duchess of Cambridge were expecting their first child. The announcement was made earlier in the pregnancy than is usual because of the Duchess's admission to hospital with hyperemesis gravidarum — a complication of early pregnancy characterized by severe nausea, vomiting, weight loss, and dehydration. At the time, Kate was around six weeks pregnant. She had been taken ill while spending the weekend at the Berkshire home of her parents, Carole and Michael Middleton. The Middletons' had known about the pregnancy for a while whereas Prince Charles and the Queen were only informed hours before she was admitted to the King Edward VII hospital in London. In the event, Kate was hospitalised for three days before she was discharged, announcing that she felt '*much better*'. It was likely she had been given anti-sickness medication. Prince Charles was quoted for the first time about the baby, saying he was '*thrilled*' at the prospect of becoming a grandfather. '*It's a very nice thought, grandfatherhood, in my old age, if I may say so, so that's splendid,*' he said. '*And I'm very glad my daughter-in-law is getting better, thank goodness.*'

In a significant break with tradition, Kate and William spent Christmas 2012 with the Middletons at their home in the village of Bucklebury rather at Sandringham with the Royals, allowing the mother-to-be to rest and relax. The Duke and Duchess affectionately referred to their unborn child as '*our little grape*' and enjoyed a New Year '*babymoon*' along with the Middletons in the Caribbean. By February 2013, the Duchess seemed to be taking pregnancy in her stride, commenting during an official function that she was now '*feeling great*' and wanted '*to stay busy*'. She was universally praised for her stylish maternity wardrobe which featured pieces from both the High Street and top-end designers. It was also revealed by '*sources*' close to the Duchess that her due date was July 13 and she had also developed a passion for lavender-flavoured biscuits! Kate's sister Pippa threw a baby shower for her a few months before the little Prince or Princess was due — the Duke and Duchess didn't wish to know the sex of their baby before he or she was born — complete with a dummy-shaped cake. As Kate's due date approached, she was apparently revelling in the final weeks of her pregnancy. '*Kate finds pregnancy fascinating,*' a source said at the time. '*She still says, "I can't believe it" when you talk about a baby being inside her".*' The insider added that Prince William was just as transfixed. '*They're both so excited and have so many questions.*' Like most first-time parents, '*they want to know what the baby will look like and who it will take after.*'

Royal baby fever really started to take hold at the beginning of July. The world's press started camping outside St Mary's Hospital in Paddington in anticipation of the Royal birth. A bay of parking spaces outside the Lindo Wing were closed off with signs saying that they were reserved for an '*event*' until July 31. On July 9, it was announced

Main Image & Below:
Prince William, Duke of Cambridge and Catherine, Duchess of Cambridge depart the Lindo Wing at St Mary's Hospital with their new born son on July 22 2013

from Buckingham Palace that, '*The Royal couple's child will officially be known as His or Her Royal Highness the Prince or Princess of Cambridge.*' On the same day, Zara Tindall, the Queen's granddaughter and Prince William's cousin, announced that she too was expecting her first baby. As the days passed and there was still no news of the birth, the phrase '*The Great Kate Wait*' was coined by an impatient media. It seemed the Royals were feeling just as frustrated. Prince Charles and Camilla continued their engagements around the country and admitted to well-wishers that they were '*all waiting at the end of the telephone*', while the Queen told one little girl during a walkabout at Lake Windermere, in Cumbria, that she hoped the baby would '*hurry up*' because she was planning to go on holiday to Balmoral. Kate finally went into labour in the early hours of Monday July 22, and she and William were driven from their home at Kensington Palace to St Mary's at around 5.30am.

At 7.30am it was announced that Kate was '*in the early stages of labour*' and that things were '*progressing normally*'. Her baby son was finally born at 4.24pm after a 10-hour labour on one of the hottest days of the year. Prince William was at her side throughout and it was thought she'd had the natural birth she so desired. The baby, third in line to the throne, weighed 8lb 6oz, had a wisp of dark hair and, according to his father, '*a good set of lungs*'. The news wasn't made public for another four hours as the couple got to know their baby, and informed family members. At around 8.30pm, a statement was issued via e-mail and Twitter, announcing the birth. It read, '*Her Royal Highness the Duchess of Cambridge was safely delivered of a son at 4.24pm*'.

The next morning the King's Troop Royal Horse Artillery fired a 41-gun salute in Green Park at the same time as a 62-gun salute at the Tower of London. Meanwhile outside St Mary's Paddington, hoards of reporters and camera crews from around the world waited for the new born and his parents to emerge. Shortly after lunchtime, Carole and Michael Middleton arrived to visit their daughter and first grandchild. Then it was the turn of Prince Charles and the Duchess of Cornwall. It was not until the evening William, Kate and their baby emerged on the same steps upon which the baby William had made his first appearance 31 years earlier. After a brief exchange with the media in which Kate revealed that William had '*already changed his first nappy*' with William adding that it was a very happy, emotional time, the new little family

Left:
Prince William holds his son, Prince George, as they arrive at St James's Palace for the three-month-old's christening on October 23 2013

Right:
Prince George plays with the his mother's hair during a visit to Government House in Wellington, New Zealand in April 2014

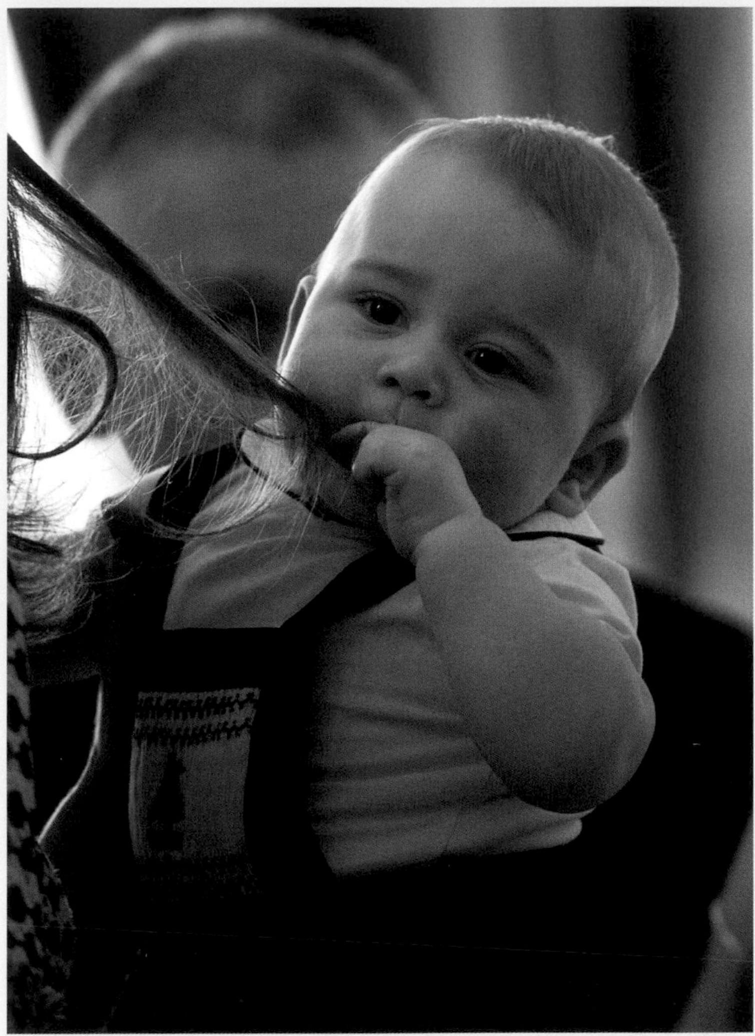

headed home to Kensington. The Queen visited her first great grandson and heir the next day — it was the first time in almost 120 years that a reigning sovereign had cradled a direct heir who was three generations down in line to the throne. The last time being when Queen Victoria held the future Edward VIII in her arms in summer 1894. The Duke and Duchess then announced their baby's name. He would be called Prince George Alexander Louis of Cambridge. George after the Queen's father, King George VI, Alexander was thought to be Kate's first choice of name for her son, and Louis as it was one of William's own names and also a tribute to Prince Charles' mentor and great uncle, Lord Louis Mountbatten.

Like many first-time mums, Kate wished to be near her own mum while she got to grips with motherhood and the next morning, she, William and George — along with their security detail — made for Bucklebury. The new parents did not wish to call in a nanny or nursery nurse to help with their new born but his doting grandparents would be on hand. For the next six weeks, Kate devoted herself to her son, although his father returned to his then-job as a RAF Helicopter Rescue Pilot after two weeks paternity leave. According to William, becoming a dad was truly life-changing. '*It's only been a short period, but a lot of things affect me differently now,*' he revealed a few weeks after George's birth. He added that Kate was doing a *'fantastic job'* with the baby, whom he described as *'a little bit of a rascal. . . . He either reminds me of my brother or me when I was younger, I'm not sure, but he's doing very well at the moment. . . . He's growing up quite quickly, actually. But he's a little fighter–he wriggles around quite a lot and he doesn't want to go to sleep that much.*' That was an understatement. By all accounts George was a very hungry baby who hardly slept, leaving his mother exhausted. By the time the family returned to Kensington Palace that autumn, William had asked one of his former nannies, Jessie Webb, to step in and help.

Prince George's next public appearance was at his christening in the Chapel of St James' Palace on October 23 2013. His godparents included the pregnant Zara Tindall and the Duke and Duchess' right hand man, Jamie Lowther-Pinkerton. Baby George wore the replica heavy satin and Honiton lace christening robe, and he was welcomed into the Christian faith with water from the River Jordan. He barely whimpered, according to reports. His Aunt Pippa read from Luke Ch.18, in which Christ says

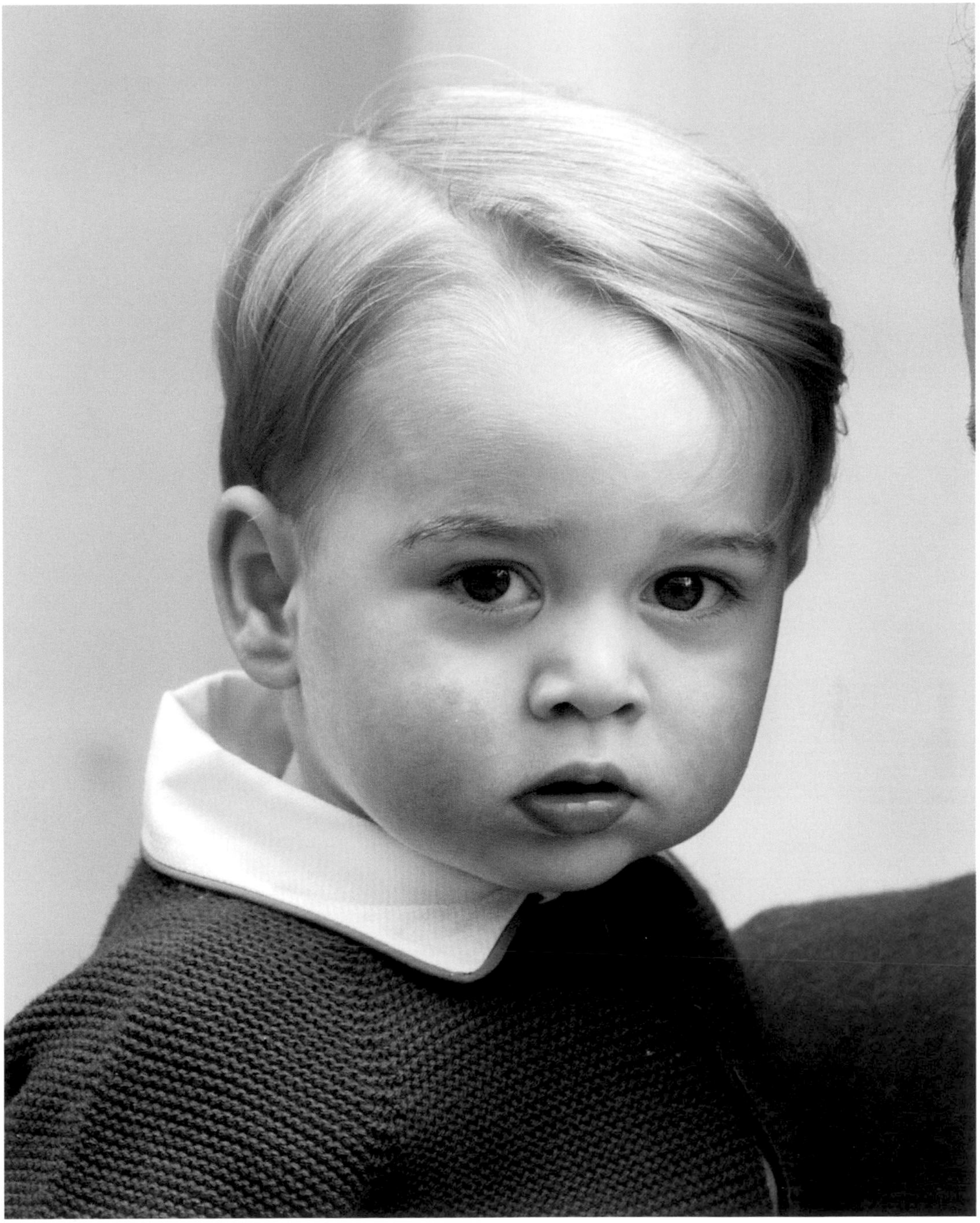

Left:

The Duchess of Cambridge and Prince George attend the Jerudong Park Trophy at Cirencester Park Polo Club on June 15 2014

Above:

Prince George arriving with his dad at the Lindo Wing, St Mary's Hospital, after the Duchess of Cambridge gave birth to Princess Charlotte on May 2 2015

Left:
Prince George plays with bubbles at a children's party for Military families during the Royal Tour of Canada on September 29 2016

'*Suffer little children to come unto me*', while his Uncle Harry read from John Ch.15, in which Jesus tells his followers to '*Abide in me, and I in you*'. After the service the small party adjourned to Clarence House for a champagne reception hosted by the Prince of Wales and Duchess of Cornwall, where they were offered slices of one of the tiers of the Duke and Duchess's wedding cake, saved for the occasion. Meanwhile the Royal Mint issued a set of commemorative coins to celebrate the christening, the first coins to mark a Royal christening in Britain.

In the spring of 2014, the Duke and Duchess of Cambridge appointed a full-time nanny in the form of Spaniard Maria Borrallo. Trained at the prestigious Norland College, she quickly became close to George and his parents, with Kate calling her '*amazing*'. Shortly after her appointment, George, with his parents and Maria, embarked on his first royal tour in April 2014, during which the Cambridges spent three weeks in New Zealand and Australia. Highlights included the eight-month old enjoying a playdate with other babies of his age at Government House, Wellington, and meeting a bilby who was named after him at Sydney Zoo. At the end of the trip, it was clear that the little Prince had stolen the show. It was also clear from the very natural and instinctive way the Duke and Duchess interacted with their son that they were the most hands-on Royal parents seen to date.

In October 2014, an incident '*prompted Their Royal Highnesses to seek reasonable assurances*' from an individual whom they've asked to stop '*harassing and following both Prince George and his nanny,*' Buckingham Palace announced. It was also requested that paparazzi desist from snapping the little Prince. Like any parents, the Duke and Duchess wanted Prince George to have the freedom to safely experience normal childhood activities like going to the park and playing with other children. Although photographs were released of Prince George, often taken by his mother, over the next months, his next public appearance was not to be until May 2015 when he arrived at St Mary's Hospital in Paddington and met his new sister for the first time.

Prince William's verdict on his baby daughter

'A little joy of heaven'

Princess Charlotte

It was announced on 8 September 2014 that the Duke and Duchess of Cambridge were expecting their second child. As with Kate's first pregnancy, the announcement was made early as she was again suffering with hyperemesis gravidarum. However, this time she was treated at home rather than hospital. Clarence House said, '*The Queen and members of both families are delighted with the news.*' And during an event for The Prince's Trust charity, Prince Charles told reporters he was '*looking forward*' to becoming a grandfather again, adding, '*I hope it will be a girl this time.*' A month later the Duke and Duchess were '*delighted to confirm they are expecting a baby girl in April 2015,*' the Palace revealed, adding that while the Duchess continued to suffer from acute morning sickness '*her condition was steadily improving.*' On October 21, Kate made her first public appearance since the announcement of her pregnancy when she welcomed the President of the Republic of Singapore to the U.K. His wife said she was glad Kate had made the engagement. '*So am I,*' Kate replied. '*I've been looking forward to getting out of the house, that's for sure!*' By early 2015, Kate mentioned during an official function that, '*It's moving all the time — I can feel it kicking now.*' As she had previously, Kate bloomed during her second trimester. '*I sometimes forget I'm pregnant,*' she was quoted as saying.

The Duchess was once again booked into the Lindo Wing at Queen Mary's Hospital in Paddington, although contingency plans were put in place. If the Duchess unexpectedly went into labour while visiting her parents in Bucklebury, she would be taken to the Royal Berkshire Hospital in Reading. While if she went into labour at Anmer Hall, the couple's country residence in Norfolk, she would give birth at the Queen Elizabeth Hospital in King's Lynn. She let slip that she was due *'mid to*

Right:
Crowds gather at Buckingham Palace after the birth of the new Princess on May 2 2015

Above:
Notice placed at Buckingham Palace after the birth of the new Princess

late April'. One clue came when notices appeared suspending parking outside the hospital from April 15-30. They were hastily extended for five days when no baby materialised. On May 2 2015 Kate was admitted to St. Mary's at 6 a.m. in London in '*the early stages of labour*'. The Cambridge's baby daughter was born just two-and-a-half hours later, delivered naturally as her elder brother had been. She weighed 8lbs 3oz and was a week overdue. Her father was present at the birth. The little Princess was fourth in line to the throne and the first Royal to benefit from changes to the law, stating that her place in the line of succession could no longer be usurped by any future younger brothers.

The official announcement came at 11.10am. Crowds outside the hospital popped Cava corks, hung up pink bunting, whooped, cheered and chanted '*Princess! Princess! Princess!*' for the hordes of assembled media. At 4pm, William emerged from the hospital, only to return a little time later with 22-month-old, Prince George. The crowds cheered wildly as the Duke carried his small son up the steps to the Lindo wing to meet his new sister, with the infant Prince being coaxed into giving a small royal wave. Replying to shouts from the media asking how he felt, William said he was '*very happy*'. The Princess returned home with her parents to Kensington Palace that evening, after a brief photocall on the steps of the Lindo Wing where she slept soundly in her mother's arms. Landmarks such as Tower Bridge, London Eye, the Trafalgar Square fountains in London and the Peace Tower in Ottawa, Ontario, were illuminated pink to mark the Princess's birth. Royal Mail commemorated the birth with an unprecedented congratulations postmark, the first time in its 500-year history it had done so, while the top of London's BT tower repeatedly scrolled the message, 'It'*s a girl*'. On 4 May, gun salutes were fired at Hyde Park and the Tower of London. Later that day, the baby girl's name was announced as Charlotte Elizabeth Diana — this last name being for William's late mother, of course.

This time around, the Cambridges employed a maternity nurse to help them through the first few months of Charlotte's life. However, unlike her brother, she was a good sleeper. When she was a month old, the Princess was photographed with her brother Prince George at Anmer Hall in Norfolk, Kate having taken the pictures herself. On 5 July 2015, she was baptised by the Archbishop of Canterbury at St. Mary Magdalene Church, Sandringham. She arrived at the church, pushed by her mother in a traditional Silver Cross pram. Her father and brother followed. The christening marked the first occasion that the Cambridges stepped out publicly as a family of four. The Duchess wore head-to-toe Alexander McQueen — as she had for George's Big Day — while George was dressed in red shorts and an embroidered top for his sister's christening. The outfit was almost identical to the one worn by William when he had been taken to meet his brother Harry for the first time. Her god parents included a maternal cousin of William's and a paternal cousin of Kate's.

Main Image & Left:
Catherine, Duchess of Cambridge and Prince William, Duke of Cambridge depart the Lindo Wing, St Mary's Hospital with their new born daughter on May 2 2015

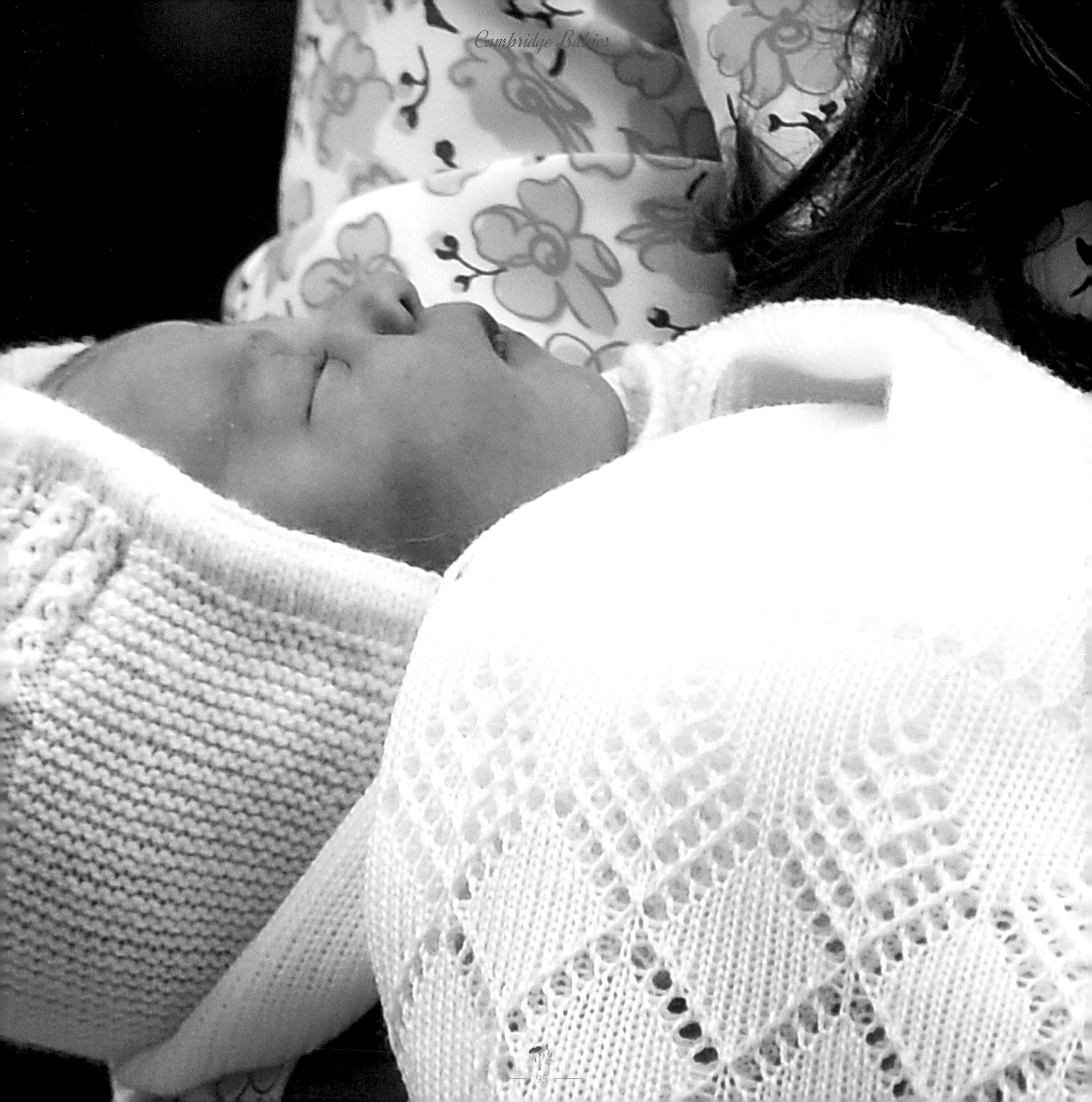

Above & Right:

Duchess of Cambridge and Princess Charlotte at a children's party for Military families during the Royal Tour of Canada on September 29 2016

When she was six-months-old, more photographs of the baby Princess, taken by her mother, were released to the world's press. An accompanying statement read, '*The Duke and Duchess continue to receive warm messages about Princess Charlotte from all around the world and they hope that everyone enjoys these lovely photos as much as they do.*' In March 2016, photos of the family on a ski break were released, with Kensington Palace revealing that, '*This was their first holiday as a family of four and the first time either of the children had played in the snow.*' Various other images of the Princess were released over the coming months such as making her first official public appearance on the balcony of Buckingham Palace for Queen Elizabeth II's Trooping the Colour ceremony in June 2016 and arriving in Canada on her first State visit with her family in September 2016. To mark her second birthday in May 2017, Kensington Palace released a picture, taken in April by her mother, the Duchess of Cambridge, at Anmer Hall in Norfolk, saying, '*Their Royal Highnesses would like to thank everyone for all of the lovely messages they have received, and hope that everyone enjoys this photograph of Princess Charlotte as much as they do.*' Both children were photographed looking angelic at the wedding of their Aunt Pippa later that month. It has become the Cambridge's policy to release images of their children — taken by their mother wherenever possible - at intervals throughout the year.

Both children have become style setters in much the same way as their mother. Prince George was ranked 49 on a '*50 Best Dressed Men in Britain*' list in 2015! The clothes in which they are photographed, immediately become best sellers. In 2016, for instance, the dressing gown Prince George sported while meeting the Obamas sold out after he was seen wearing it. The Princess Charlotte effect is even more apparent. '*Demand for items Princess Charlotte wears will surge massively on our site,*' explains a representative from online childrenswear shop Alex and Alexa. '*We saw an increase in customers*

Left:
Duchess of Cambridge speaks to Princess Charlotte after the wedding of Pippa Middleton and James Matthews at St Mark's Church, Englefield Greed on May 20 2017

Above & Left:

Princess Charlotte & Prince George fulfilling their duties at the wedding of Pippa Middleton and James Matthews at St Mark's Church, Englefield Green on May 20 2017

searching for pale pink cardigans and floral dresses after the first shots of Princess Charlotte were released and this grew again after the release of the adorable shot of The Queen with her great grandchildren.' Experts at Brand Finance have predicted that Charlotte will be worth more than £3 billion to the UK economy across her lifetime.

When it comes to raising their growing family, The Duke and Duchess are mindful to teach good wellbeing awareness to their children with William commenting, '*Catherine and I are clear that we want both George and Charlotte to grow up feeling able to talk about their emotions and feelings.*' Such sentiments would see Queens Victoria and Mary turning in their graves! The parents are also breaking some rules when it comes to educating their offspring. For instance, Prince George is attending Thomas's Battersea co-ed school, unlike William and Prince Harry who went to all-boys Wetherby School. As to the children's personalities, their father has described his son as '*a monkey*' while adding that his daughter is '*a little joy of heaven*'. However, it was the Queen who revealed that little sister Princess Charlotte loves to look after big brother Prince George. When presenting a children's prize at Sandringham, Her Majesty asked a

Main Image:
The Duke of Cambridge, Duchess of Cambridge, Prince George of Cambridge and Princess Charlotte of Cambridge arrive at Berlin Tegel Airport during an official visit to Poland and Germany on July 19 2017

10-year-old girl whether she '*looked after*' her little sister. When the child's mother replied that it was the other way around, the Queen remarked, '*It's like that with Charlotte and George.*' Kate has also inferred that it is Charlotte who ruled the nursery roost, declaring that the toddler was '*the one in charge*'.

For Cambridge baby number three, we can expect more of the same, although it has been mooted that Kate would love a home birth at either Kensington Palace or Anmer House this time around. As a mother, she has been more open and honest than any other Royal in history. '*It is a wonderful and rewarding experience,*' she recently remarked, '*however, at times it has also been a huge challenge — even for me, who has support at home that most mothers do not. Nothing can really prepare you for the sheer overwhelming experience of what it means to become a mother. It is full of complex emotions of joy, exhaustion, love and worry, all mixed together. Your fundamental identity changes overnight. You go from thinking of yourself as primarily an individual, to suddenly being a mother, first and foremost. For many mothers, myself included, this can, at times, lead to lack of confidence and feelings of ignorance. And yet there is no rule book …*

… You just have to make it up and do the very best you can to care for your family.'